UP THE GARDEN PATH

A short memoir on opening a garden
for the National Garden Scheme

By

HENRY BUTTERFIELD

The Dedication

To the National Garden Scheme for all the fantastic work they do in raising millions of pounds every year for several worthy charities, including Marie Curie and Macmillan nurses, but not forgetting the annual guest charity. And of course, we mustn't forget all those selfless gardeners who open up their gardens to the viewing public. Once again thank you.

❀

To my long-suffering wife, Evelyn. The Lady of the Garden who supports our gardening efforts and puts up with all the mad-brained ideas of her old fart of a husband. Evelyn, I love you and thanks a million.

To my dear friend Ken

I hope you enjoy this little book

Your old mate

Henry

Authors Note.

Although this is a work of non-fiction, some of the names have been changed, and some characters and events merged together as is common practice in memoir writing so as to make the book interesting. Also, because of legal requirements, the names of the production company and the national television broadcasting company have been changed (or ignored) as necessary. Dialogue, when it comes naturally, is usually extremely boring, hard to follow and looks ghastly on the printed page. Therefore, where needed, it has been jazzed up a bit. If you want to see the programme with its warts and all, keep an eye open for any repeats the television may have to offer.

Books by the same author:

Well, none as yet, but keep your eyes open, more'll be along d'rectly, as they say in Devon.

CHAPTER ONE

THE THREE YEAR PLAN
(Sounds a bit Russian doesn't it?)

'Henry, what have we taken on?'

'A lot of hard work Evelyn,' I sighed. 'I hope we can do something with it.'

That bright spring afternoon, my wife and I looked down into our new garden from the small raised veranda by the back door as though surveying the scene from the bridge of a ship. There, stretched out in a flat panorama before us, lay a middling sized town garden. It was about the size of two allotments in total. In wide-eyed dismay, we slowly realised the immensity of the task the future held.

To call it a garden was a misnomer. In reality it was an expanse of wasteland. Here and there thickets of brambles erupted, while sturdy clumps of stinging nettles stood around like mini forests. These, along with thick tuffets of coarse grass, made up our own Serengeti. It was as though great herds of Wildebeest and Maasai tribesmen could be expected to cross the plain at any moment.

The thickets were not huge, but they were big enough and well rooted enough for anyone to see that they were not going to yield their ground easily. The thought of having a ruined back by the time they had been removed was not particularly appealing. How long it would take to clear the stinging nettles was anybody's guess, and what grass there was would never make a lawn again. Whatever glory days those traces of green had enjoyed were gone forever. This garden would have to start from scratch.

Numerous sheets of rusty, buckled, corrugated iron lay on and in the ground. An investigation was needed. On lifting the sheets, it was surprising to see families of slow worms warming themselves in the radiated heat of the metal. Never before had I seen so many in one place, every sheet had their quota of them. Unfortunately, after this disturbance, they disappeared.

They were rediscovered hibernating later on during the winter. On entering the shed at the bottom of the garden, they were crammed into the roof cavities where the roof joins the top of the walls. There were scores of them, literally hanging there, all squashed together like rush hour commuters on the London underground. It was interesting to note that they were as skilled at climbing as they were at crawling.

It is a shame, but what appeared to be a wilderness to us humans, happened to be the perfect, paradisiacal, idyll to Mr and Mrs Slow worm and family. The development of the garden must have upset them to the core, because in just a matter of two years they had all but disappeared to more accommodating territory. There was the occasional sighting of the odd one or two by the pond or in the compost heap, but now we never see any at all.

This experience aroused my interest in wildlife proper and caused me to find out more about this gentle creature.

To begin with, the term slow worm is a thoroughly inaccurate description of this attractive reptile, because, 1) it isn't slow, it is in fact rather swift across the ground, and 2) it isn't a worm, it's a limbless lizard. It's a strange thing with us British; we often give flora and fauna such inappropriate common names, sometimes for no apparent reason.

Sadly, the slow worm, along with many other forms of wildlife, has suffered badly in this country over the past decades. Generally, it's all because people, who like me, often unthinkingly, occasionally in ignorance, but sometimes deliberately, ride roughshod over their habitat. We tidy our gardens, and spray all manner of poisons onto them without considering the eco-system. The slow worms taught a salutary lesson here. Before any action is undertaken, we should study our garden and analyse its own unique eco-system before blundering ahead and destroying the delicate balance that may already exist. An element of sensitivity certainly would not go amiss when garden planning.

On examination, the slow worm (*Anguis fragilis*) looks much like a small snake. There is a vast variety of colouration that is affected by the age, and gender, of the creature. Individuals do have unique markings, although overall they sport a brown or grey metallic shine.

They differ from snakes in a number of ways. Firstly, it may be surprising to know that slow worms have eyelids. Patient close inspection will be rewarded with a sudden flash of eyelid as they blink. Look even closer and you may also see their tiny ears, another sign that they are not snakes. Furthermore, they can perform that remarkable trick that every schoolboy of old has heard of, autotomy; the miraculous act of shedding the tail to escape predators. The tail does regrow but it never has the quality of the original. It has a dumpy look about it making it easy to spot an individual who has had a close shave with something that thought it would be a good lunch. Rather than lay eggs like a snake, this lizard has a viviparous birth; it gives birth to live young. When born they are in the region of seven to ten centimetres long, and when full grown can reach as much as 45 centimetres.

Slow worms can live a long time too. It is estimated that in the wild, the occasional individual can make it to about 30 years old, although in captivity they can live much longer. The oldest known specimen was a male who reached the ripe old age of 54 (1892-1946) and was a resident of Copenhagen Zoo.

Slow worms perform nothing but good deeds in the garden. They keep the gardener's enemies at bay by consuming copious amounts of slugs and suchlike related nasties. They can be encouraged to take up residence if roofing slates or small pieces of metal are placed strategically around the garden and are supported on little stones (or shale in our case – you will see why shortly.) This will tempt them to sun themselves and to live in the shelter of its damp shade. A compost heap and pond will benefit them too.

So, why have we had all this prattle about slow worms? Well, it was this episode with them that changed my outlook on gardening style and philosophy. Thinking back to that time from the position I find myself in now, it still fills me with a touch of sadness. I would have been handled it differently if it was possible to do so, but at that time I was not into wildlife gardening. Like so many people, I was caught up in my own existence; I never gave wildlife much thought at all. It was something that looked after itself, on the periphery of human activity, as though it was on the same, but a different planet. Goodness, how we alter over the years, how our viewpoints do change, how we become more reflective about our lives and our place in the world around us. Time has shown that on the whole, as a species, we are exploiters; we are powerful, manipulative, and selfish. We use our strength to take advantage of, and dominate our environment to its detriment. I never knew how strongly I would feel about this when I later became 'wildlife aware.'

❀❀❀

These thoughts of wildlife gardening were for future years though. The beast that was the back garden still had to be brought to order. A closer investigation of our urban Serengeti exhibited ominous humps and bumps rippling across the surface of the ground. Scraping back the soil revealed that these eruptions were even more sheets of subterranean corrugated iron. So, not only was there hard work on top, there was more hard work lying underground.

A soil examination gave the situation even greater meaning. I picked up a handful of earth and let it run like water through my fingers, the texture was ominous. It felt sandy and light. Was this going to be a blessing or a curse? Would it be free draining and warm up quickly in the spring, or would it dry out with the slightest glow of the sun and become a baked and impoverished dust bowl?

To learn more about the soil, I took my fork and pricked around with it, breaking the ground's thin greyish crust. Even worse was waiting to be discovered. A few centimetres below the surface was a stratum of broken shillet, (a Devonian term for shale.) It was as though a rustic building had been demolished and a thin layer of fine soil had been sprinkled on top. Every time the fork entered the ground the prongs constantly struck this shale with an unnerving twang of the tines.

This dastardly shillet did not lay hidden alone though. It had many formidable allies with it. Besides those dreaded corrugated iron sheets, along came other detritus such as brickbats, iron bedsteads, numerous other metal relics from times past, pieces of china crockery, and torn and ripped polythene sheeting.

Our southern neighbour, Mrs Long, was in her garden happily hanging out her washing. She glanced over the fence into our wilderness.

'Bit of a mess isn't it?' she commented in her Devonshire burr.

'It is rather,' I said looking back at her.

'People used to keep chickens there for years. Chicken coops everywhere; nothing else much.'

'Oh.'

'They pretty well used the rest of the garden as a midden.' She waved her finger at it.

'So I see.'

'Enjoy your garden won't you,' she smiled. With that Mrs Long picked up her washing basket, turned on her heels, and went back indoors.

One moment's reflection showed that this was going to be a laborious, long drawn out process. There was going to be no quick fix. But where should we begin?

❀❀❀

To paraphrase, Do-re-mi, from the Sound of Music, we thought it a good idea to start at the very beginning. Why? Because it's a very good place to start; when you sing you begin with do-re-mi, but when you garden you begin with a plan you see (well it rhymes, sort of.) And so that's what we accepted. As mentioned previously, this garden was going to a long term venture; therefore, head work was needed before hard work.

For many evenings during the course of that summer we sat at the dining room table with scraps of paper and propelling pencils trying to decide what course to follow. The problem was that starting a garden from scratch is often more problematical than redeveloping an existing garden. Even if it's not to your taste, or is overgrown, at least there is some kind of structure. Everything else, the plants, and the shrubs, can be kept under control or moved. In the process, the garden can be slowly transformed, to be reawakened like a sleeping beauty.

We played with any number of ideas and drew many sketches, all of which ended in the waste paper basket. Then, totally by chance, we happened to put on the television for the lunchtime news and discovered the late, great, Geoff Hamilton expounding the merits of his Ornamental Kitchen Garden in his television series of the same name.

We bought the book and were totally enthralled by the idea of growing ornamentals and vegetables together. It was a modern take on the old-fashioned pottager gardens. It seemed such a natural thing to do. And Geoff was fully organic so there were no pesticides, no herbicides, no poisons whatsoever. Therefore, after talking it over, it was decided that we would become good old-fashioned cottage gardeners, and do that very thing. We eventually bought all Geoff's books until he died of a heart attack while on a charity cycle ride event.

As plans continued to be made during that hot summer, we recognised that the project would take at least three years. We had our ideas on plan, but now they needed to be put into action. And, in time, we would fully understand the truth of Rudyard Kipling's 'Glory of the Garden,' where he states… 'such gardens are not made, by saying, "Oh how wonderful" and sitting in the shade.'

❀❀❀

As it stood, the front and the side of the house were appalling. The area looked like a bomb site. The reclamation was long and arduous because of the shillet that gave the impression that it lived and grew in the soil. That blessed shale would, in the end, become the defining mark of this garden. Steady progress was made as the ground was slowly cleared and piles of shillet were assembled in strategic places, ready for the plans Evelyn had cunningly devised for them. They stood around imitating small cairns.

Running parallel to the pavement at the front of the garden was the public face of our property. This face being an old decrepit chain-link fence held up by eight centimetres square concrete posts set in huge lumps of sunken concrete. A galvanised one-metre-wide pedestrian gate was the only thing that pierced this bent and buckled monstrosity. This eyesore of a fence had to go.

❀ ❀ ❀

Enter Vernon, the husband of a friend of ours. He was a real Devonian with black hair, dark eyes, and a rich West Country burr of an accent. He wasn't a tall man, but had the strength of Sampson, and earned his living as a builder. Originally, he was just going to remove the chain-link fence, but as is the way of things, after he had finished his cup of tea with Evelyn, he went away with a front garden shopping list full of tasks.

Firstly, he would remove the fence, and then he would build a short length of concrete block wall along the boundary of Mrs Long's front garden. Next he would construct a decorative screen block wall on the raised platform that existed in front of the lounge window. This was level with the steps leading up to the front door and had a drop of about 60 centimetres into the garden. Finally, he would lay a short length of concrete to begin the entrance of our driveway.

I thought the removal of the fence would be an onerous task, but not for Vernon. From the back of his Ford Escort van, he hauled a powerful jackhammer. A job that I thought would take over a week using a pick-axe and brute force was completed in a matter of hours. This was heady stuff. Things were happening at a giddy speed.

In three days the job was complete. The front garden was now clear of the awful chain-link fence, the boundary wall was standing proud, the beginning of the new driveway was a slab of glistening grey concrete, and the screen block wall gave the whole front garden a Mediterranean feel. We were excited; our journey had begun with a positive flourish.

✵✵✵

Watching Vernon exercise his craftsmanship with sand, cement, water, and concrete blocks emboldened me to test my own skills at wall and slab building. I had a yearning to erect the front wall where it joined the pavement. All that was needed was to lay a small foundation, build the wall four blocks high, then finish off with some coping stones, and complete the job with a splatter type render. What could be more straightforward?

Well, in hindsight, learning to be a brain surgeon is probably simpler. It began well enough. Progress was fast and carefree. The trench for the foundation came out easily. Soon the bottom of the trench was level and ready to receive the footings. Confidence was high. After all, what was concrete but a recipe, and the hired cement mixer but a scaled up Kenwood Chef? All one had to do was to throw in the ingredients, let it mix for a while, turn it into the wheelbarrow, and then use, just like icing on a cake.

But then water came into the picture. Never underestimate the importance of water in making concrete. It is the magic of the mix. Too little, and the consistency is so dry that it will not hold together, it just falls apart into crumbs. Too much, and the concrete flows like cold molten volcanic lava, useful for nothing. And a thimbleful of water can make all the difference.

Unfortunately, I'm not the most patient person in the world, and this was reflected in my concrete mixing and the addition water. I began cautiously at first, unsure of how much to put in. First a splash was added, then another splash, and then yet another splash.

This, the deep drone of the motor, and the constant pulse of the mixer drum as it churned the contents over and over created a hypnotic effect, especially so as the afternoon was hot and balmy. Suddenly, in a trancelike state, I lost my patience and impulsively threw in half a bucket of water. Instantly, what appeared to damp grey sand became a runny grey gloop. The suddenness of the change was startling. More sand and cement was immediately shovelled in only to see it dry out again. The lesson learned, water continued to be added by the cupful rather than by the bucket. Sorry to say that at the end of the exercise, there was twice the amount of concrete than was needed for the job.

It never ceases to surprise me the way knock-on effects form a chain of events that slowly build into an increasing feeling of panic, especially when outside circumstances join in to conspire against you. One of those arch conspirators was the weather. That summer was hot. There was little wind and the atmosphere lay on the garden like a heavy blanket. One could sense the water evaporating from the ground like the drying of lakes. It didn't bode well.

The first length of foundation went into the trench comfortably. But, as time wore on the sun began to have an ill effect on the concrete that remained. It started to go off before my eyes. Its colour lightened by the minute; it became a race against the clock. There was another short stretch of foundation to dig while preventing that concrete from setting. After a quick rummage in the shed a piece of old sacking was found and hastily made wet. It was not a moment too soon because the edge of the concrete in the wheelbarrow had already become crispy. However, the damp sacking and copious sprinklings of water saved the mixture from spoiling, but to quote Wellington at Waterloo, it was a close run thing.

When the foundations had set it was time to progress to building the concrete block wall. This was yet another steep learning curve. The dexterity of the mason and his control of the trowel is a masterpiece; no wonder a person accomplished in this art is called a master mason. Obvious to say, I did not have these skills and would be more accurately known as a rubbish mason. As the blocks were laid, the mortar would not adhere to them for love nor money. As one block was laid against the previous one, the mixture kept falling off. It happened repeatedly and was vexing until a way was improvised to get the mortar between them. The final resort was to hold a flat piece of plywood against one side of the gap and to fill the space by poking in the mixture with a trowel, and then making it compact with a thin piece of batten. On completion there was almost as much mortar running along the base of the new wall as there was holding it all together, and the joints were ugly as Eli Wallach, and as thick as a plank. (Try doing a Google search for Eli and you'll see what I mean.)

Just as I was tidying up, another local builder named Dick came strolling down the road as though he had no cares in the world; which I guess he didn't because he was always the jovial sort. He stopped, rolled the remains of his Rizla roll up cigarette from one side of his mouth to the other, pushed his battered old trilby up from his forehead and made his observations on my handiwork.

'You been laying they there blocks boy?' he asked in a strong Devonshire dialect.

'I have Dick.' I said, standing back and presenting my work with a flourish of the hand. 'What do you think?'

'Tisn't bad for a beginner I suppose.' His eyes stared at the wall. 'You've used a pretty thick layer of mortar 'tween them there blocks though.'

'Yes I know. But it's a difficult thing to handle, this mortar, cement, concrete, or whatever you want to blimming well call it. It's ghastly stuff.'

'Don't knock it boy. It's been around a long time.' He paused. 'And it changed the world.'

Dick had one of his knowledgeable looks on his face so I had a feeling that one of his lectures was about to bubble forth. I immediately excused myself to make us a cup of tea. If there was some learning to be done, then it would be madness not to be comfortable while learning it.

When I returned with a tray of tea and biscuits, Dick was sitting on the doorstep with a new chalk white 'rolly' in his mouth, and a plume of smoke drifting lazily into the atmosphere. He looked at me from the corner of his eye and smiled.

'Do you know who invented concrete?'

'No idea.' I replied.

'Them there Romans. They discovered pozzolana cement.'

'What's that when it's home?'

'The same stuff as when it's not at home. It's volcanic ash. They found it at Pozzuoli.' He paused for a moment. 'That's why it's called pozzolana cement.'

'Logical I suppose.'

'Yea. And they added lime. That's not lime as in the fruit of course, but lime as in… lime.' He paused again. 'Anyway, they added this lime and sand to make it into a good concrete mixture. But, not only that boy, here's another thing, how about this? From time to time, they also added things like milk, fat, blood and stuff!'

'Is that right? Did it work?'

'You bet it did. A lot of they things them Romans built are still around us today you know.' He began to run off a list. 'There's the Appian Way. That's the road that runs south from Rome and was the first stretch of paved road in the history of man.'

'Get on.'

'Yea, that's right boy. They also used it to build them there Roman baths that were so popular. It kept the pools watertight. Then there's that Coliseum, where they had all them gladiators and the fighting going on.' A thoughtful look came across his face. 'Though mind you, I wouldn't think there was much to be glad about if you was a gladiator. Proper miss-naming that be. Anyway, and of course there's the Pantheon. That's a famous temple place what's dedicated to a pantheon of gods. That's how it got its name you see.'

'That's interesting.'

'Yea, but strangely enough, in the dark ages the quality of cement went downhill. But, then, in the 1600s it gradually improved until in 1824 a chap called Joseph Aspdin, not Aspirin as in the painkiller, but Aspdin, he made an even greater discovery.'

'Did he now?'

'Yea, he took limestone and clay and burned it in a limekiln until the carbon dioxide was expelled. The resulting lumps were ground down with gypsum into a powder and the outcome was Portland cement.'

'That's this stuff.' I pointed to the dusty, buff coloured bags lying in the driveway.

'Yea, Portland cement is the most used general purpose cement around, and it's the basic ingredient in the majority of concrete and mortar used today.'

Our conversation continued for some time as I learned about the way concrete hardens, that the word concrete comes from the Latin word *concretus* which means "hard," and that concrete is the most used man-made material in the world, with China using the lion's share.

Eventually, Dick wound up his dissertation on the history of cement and concrete. Judging by his expression, he was feeling good with himself.

'How come you know all that stuff, Dick?' I asked.

'I'm applying for Mastermind, boy. The history of cement and concrete is going to be my specialist subject.'

'I guessed it might.' I paused and then said, 'Do you know that you start nearly every comment with 'yea'? It might be an idea to try and think of something else if you're going to be on TV.'

'Yea, good thinking boy.'

With that he got up from the step, thanked me for the tea and biscuits, said cheerio, and then proudly wandered off down the street with a swaying gait. I remained sitting there, duly enlightened.

Now it may seem strange to discuss concrete in a garden memoir, but it is surprising how many tons of it we actually use. It's used for the foundation of garden buildings, for postholes, for walls, for paths, for ornaments, for ponds, for pots, and for laying slabs. It's even used for nest boxes now. It's become an integral part of gardening as much as bamboo canes and compost.

❀ ❀ ❀

The remaining project for the rest of that summer was to complete the driveway and to finish the front garden. In the process, another lesson in the mastery of concrete would be learned; only this time it would involve the ratios of sand, cement, and a new ingredient to me, aggregate.

Carrying on with the driveway went fine until the cement began to run low. I couldn't be bothered to break off and go to the builder's merchants for more, so I tried to eke it out. Big mistake. The resultant mixture was too sandy and stony by far. It went down fine when it was wet and looked okay as it dried. And it did serve its purpose for a while. But, as it aged over the coming months, the rain slowly eroded the thin concrete from the surface. Gradually the aggregate became exposed and, in places, the driveway began to turn to dust. There was not enough cement in the mixture to hold it together. It was too weak. Cutting corners created an unmitigated disaster, and necessitated running repairs over the following years. The moral of the story? Simple. Do not scrimp on materials; it costs more money and time in the end.

❀ ❀ ❀

The summer wore on and we decided that the front garden should be completed as soon as possible. In went buff coloured concrete (there's that word again) edging strips to create two small beds, one on each side of the pedestrian gate. In each of these, we planted a cherry tree, the beautiful columnar Japanese flowering cherry, *Prunus 'Amanogawa,'* which can ultimately reach six metres tall with a spread of two metres. In spring, its young leaves give a bronze-green backdrop to the sumptuous shrimp-pink flowers that heave with bees and other valuable insects. In the autumn, as the sugars turn to starch in the leaves, the lemon yellow and crimson red foliage beset the eye. It is a breath-taking sight when seen from the road. These magnificent trees eventually gave the house and garden its name, "Cherry Trees." Beneath them, as under-planting, went winter and spring flowering heathers of the *Erica carnea* and *Erica x darlyensis* type.

The laying of buff coloured shingle, planted with more of those cheerful heathers, almost completed the front garden project. These heaths were chosen because they are tolerant of a hint of lime in the soil and give a pleasing show when nothing much else is in bloom. Early flying bees and insects find them a life saver.

❀ ❀ ❀

There was one more feature needed to finish the season. So once more out came the cement mixer and in came more concrete blocks. Down went my bank balance, and up went a gated wall to separate the main garden from the driveway. It was up to my usual standard. Each end of the wall was in the right place, but the route between them was rather bowed. When viewed from the front and back, it was a work of art, but when sighted along its length it was a beautiful shallow arc like the profile of a medieval longbow. That yet another lesson learned; always use a builder's line and never trust your eye. Nevertheless, on went a coat of white exterior paint to brighten it up, and a wooden gate was hung on the side of the house for access to the garden from the drive.

❀ ❀ ❀

As winter yielded its grip the following spring, the second season's project began. This was to clear and dig from the new gated driveway wall to half way down the rest of the garden. It was hard and tiring work. Fork, spade, pickaxe, mattock, loppers, secateurs, and a wheelbarrow with a pneumatic tyre were the principle weapons in the warfare against the underground detritus and over ground brimbles and dashles (Devon colloquialisms for brambles and thistles.)

The brambles stood like proud fountains, their multitudinous stems arching from the rootstock like jets of green and brown water spray. Their roots were thick and knobbly, (a bit like me really) and seemed to be reaching as far underground as the stems did above it. The dense grass tussocks sat proudly in the prairie, like miniature pampas grasses on the Argentinean plains. Expanses of thin parched areas held their quota of dry, brown, stiff grass whose wiry string like roots would take some removing.

That blessed shillet was still in plentiful supply. As in the previous year, the shale was accumulated into small heaps until there were kilos of the darn stuff. The Lady of the Garden was positive that it would come in handy for something architectural or showy.

Nevertheless, fine progress was made and by mid-summer that plan was well ahead of itself. Enthused by this success, extra projects were excitedly added to the list. A terrace, a pond, and an embryonic shrubbery became priority tasks.

Make no mistake; building the terrace was heavy work. Veering on the side of economy (a part time postman's wage wasn't that much) we opted for sixty centimetres square grey concrete slabs (there's that word concrete again) rather than the forty-five centimetre square reconstituted stone ones, which were considerably dearer. These hefty slabs easily weighed as much as a bag of cement and because of that were difficult to lie properly. They were laid on five concrete molehills, one in each corner, and one in the middle. The job felt like it took weeks, but in reality it was soon completed although my back and legs ached for days afterwards.

Anticipation for constructing the pond was immense. Water means life to a garden, and is an essential addition to any design. Evelyn and I enjoy auctions and by chance one day we happened to be at the local auction house when a pond was offered. It measured one hundred and fifty by ninety centimetres, and had three different depths. Unfortunately, it was the preformed rigid variety with steep sides. Although contrary to the bad press that these types of pond engender it was found that with a little bit of ingenuity in creating access routes for the residents and egress routes for those fell in accidentally, the pond was excellent.

Over the years, the pond took on its own momentum and slowly became a wildlife haven. First arrivals were the frogs and their spawn. The newts quickly followed. On their tail were damsel flies, pond skaters, and the occasional water boatman. This was another sub-liminal trigger to my interest in wildlife gardening.

It didn't take long to learn how essential it is to be picky when choosing pond plants. We put in some real bullies. On hindsight it was a bad move to put in the yellow flag iris (*Iris pseudoacorus*) even though the wildlife enjoyed it. Although stately and attractive, it is an invasive plant and quickly fills a small pond. In just three seasons, the pond was so clogged and overcrowded we had to clear it. Our experiment with the bulrush, (the Americans call them cattails, but for the life of me I can't see any similarity) wasn't wise either. In fact, the speed of invasion was even faster.

The lesson learned was that scale does matter. It is prudent to content oneself with the small, neater species. We discovered a useful water lily of modest proportions, *Nymphaea 'Frobelii.'* Only ninety centimetres across, but with beautiful ruby-red flowers and pale green leaves, it made an attractive picture. The pads were used enthusiastically by insect life throughout the summer.

During this time, we began to develop the shrubbery. Kind people kept giving us plants to help fill in the spaces. And, because we belonged to The National Trust, whenever we visited a property, we always bought a plant to remind us of the visit. This had developed into something of a vice by now, because no matter what garden we went round, even a National Garden Scheme garden, we could not resist buying a plant… or three. The daft thing about all this is that as time passes, the labels disappear, our minds dull, and we slowly forget what specific plant it is and which garden it came from anyway. But, it's just something gardeners do. We love plants and it takes a great deal of self-control to resist them.

While I concentrated on the heavy work of laying the terrace and constructing the pond, Evelyn tried a few basic vegetables in the ground that was cleared in the spring. Visible progress was now being made. After all the hard work of that summer, something tangible could be seen. It made us feel upbeat and positive for the future.

❁ ❁ ❁

We were still in good spirits when we started our third spring. At last there was light at the end of the tunnel. We were determined that this would be the last summer of deep digging and heavy heaving. And to make sure that it would be so, we got our heads down and went for completion. The final pile of shillet was made, the final piece of metal was dragged screaming and fighting from the ground. Fences were erected where necessary, paths were laid and flowerbeds prepared. Archways appeared at strategic places and a cheap and cheerful arbour was constructed of trellis at the bottom of the garden.

We wanted to create hedges but the cost of individual plants for the amount we needed would have been prohibitive. One afternoon, we were walking the dogs and turning this over in our mind when serendipity suddenly smiled upon us. We turned a corner as we passed a local factory and there, spread before us was horticultural bounty. Just that morning contractors had cut the hedge that enclosed the building. We couldn't believe what was all over the pavement. We immediately collected bulging handfuls of escallonia trimmings and bits of a silver leaved poplar type of shrub that I couldn't identify then and still can't identify now, and proudly brought them home. We promptly had scores of cuttings in pots and grew them on to maturity. It wasn't many years before they were a thriving hedge at the bottom of the garden, and a cosy shelter around the arbour.

From this, a substantial planting plan ensued. Seeds were sown, young plants grown on, and even more plants donated to the cause by kind hearted friends helped to fill the wide open spaces.

The three-year plan was achieved after a fashion, and on the whole, along the lines that Geoff Hamilton suggested. But, would it work out as envisioned?

CHAPTER TWO

DEVELOPMENTS

(And ultimate freedom!)

'The best laid schemes o' mice an' men gang aft a-gley. An' lea'e us nought but grief an' pain for promised joy.' These words of Robbie Burns proved so true over the next few years. It was soon discovered that nothing ever goes according to plan in gardening, or very rarely at least.

To begin with, the Ornamental Kitchen Garden idea didn't take off; it crashed and burned with great aplomb. The art of growing vegetables among flowers and shrubs was never truly mastered, and keeping the ground covered and filled was next to impossible. Sympathetic as we were to this principle it just wasn't going to happen on this plot no matter how much effort was put into it. That was one scheme that "gang a-gleyed." Therefore, it was back to normal gardening, although the structure and lay out of the garden from the original Geoff Hamilton plan still remains today.

The left hand side of the garden began to lend itself to a natural vegetable plot. It was open, sunny, and was at the top of the slight slope of the garden so it would not be a frost pocket. The feel of a Victorian walled garden is cosy, comfortable, and feels a little bit retro, so we surrounded it with open trellis fencing. Okay, it wasn't exactly a real walled garden, but with a lot of imagination it sufficed. It was divided it into four sections. One to hold a polythene greenhouse, which was nothing more than a short, house-shaped, polytunnel, and the other three plots were to facilitate a small crop rotation of roots, brassicas, and legumes.

Besides being a virtue, the top of the slope was also a vice. It could never be imagined just how exposed the site was. During the winter, a biting wind would rush between the houses to the southwest, and the vegetable garden turned into a wind tunnel. For three consecutive years, our polythene greenhouse took a thrashing and was destroyed each time. And for three consecutive springs, we put up another one.

Eventually, we decided not to challenge nature but to try and rub along with it instead. We took the hint and re-sited the greenhouse in a more sheltered position adjacent to the arbour. We decided to make it an aluminium glass greenhouse too, not polythene. Thankfully, there has been no trouble since.

❀ ❀ ❀

At this point, Tom Hewins, a friend of ours, came on the scene. He was a perfectionist, physically strong, not very bright academically, but kindly, and would do anything for anyone. He had a number of idiosyncrasies, one of which was a strange time-keeping habit. He didn't follow the usual routines of life as most people do, and could be relied upon to turn up to for work at any time of day. On one occasion, when he was doing some plumbing for us, we were watching television and thinking of retiring for the night when there was a knock at the door. On answering the call, I opened the door and there he stood. He had arrived to start work at 10 o'clock at night, as though it was the most normal thing in the world. He called it a day at 2.30 in the morning leaving two extremely tired householders yearning for their bed.

His kindness was such that when he heard we had acquired our greenhouse he turned up unexpectedly one afternoon and said he had some spare time and would like to erect the greenhouse for us. Taken aback by his sudden arrival and offer, we asked him how much he wanted for the job and he said that he wanted to do it as a favour for the things that we had done for him in the past. We couldn't think of anything out of the ordinary that we had done for him but once he had made up his mind that was it. As ever, he literally put his back into it. When mixing the concrete (there's that word again) for the foundation of the greenhouse, he did it all with a shovel and a mixing board by hand. No powered concrete mixer for him. It must have been hard and tiring work, but he stuck at it and the job was done perfectly and for free.

Tom was on hand when I managed to acquire a handsome second-hand eight feet by eight feet square summerhouse. This was to replace the arbour, which by now was not adequate for our needs. This summerhouse was destined to become my outdoor study, which we call the 'doghouse' today. Tom put that together too, although I had to pay him for this job. And as expected, he did it perfectly and in stages and at various times of the day or night.

Another friend of ours, Ronnie "The Rocket" Wilberforce, helped us out by erecting a porch to protect our back door from the elements. He did well with the remit we gave him, especially as at that time we didn't have much money. It had a pent roof and exterior walls of horizontal strips of wood. We named it "the signal box" because of its appearance.

Unfortunately, it faced west, directly into the prevailing weather. As a result, it leaked like a ship full of woodworm. We mentioned it to Tom, and lo and behold, he turned up shortly after with rolls of lead. In no time at all, the problem was solved.

Tom could turn his hand to anything of a constructive nature. He was not articulate and got into many a muddle with his words, but give him a practical construction problem and his mind was a sharp as a grafter's knife. And the result would be as perfect as his craftsman's hands could make it. We lost him to asbestosis in the prime of his life, his early sixties. All who knew Tom miss him still.

Another winter wind destroyed the trellis that surrounded the vegetable garden. So, as we did with the greenhouse, we decided that it was time for a more resilient structure to be erected. With no Tom to call on, we enlisted the services of Ronnie "the Rocket" once again. We removed the remnant of the wrecked trellis and 'Rocket' replaced it with a four feet high concrete block wall to create the impression of a Victorian walled garden. This was a good move because it made the exposed garden a suntrap and protected the vegetables from the worst of the westerlies.

We also lost "Rocket" to illness. His last days were uncomfortable and sad as he died of pancreatic cancer, by coincidence, just as his father had done, but he kept positive to the end. His gregarious nature, open heartedness, and generosity of spirit are still remembered by all who knew him.

⊛⊛⊛

As the years progressed, there was no real planting strategy. Plants were acquired as and when friends gave us some, or if we visited National Trust properties or gardens. The Royal Horticultural Society garden Rosemoor, at Torrington, became a regular haunt (and to be honest, it still is.) There were a number of accidental surprises with our plants. On one occasion, imported topsoil sprang us a real revelation. That summer a single seed of oilseed rape germinated. Out of interest, we left it to grow and it turned into something vast and unexpectedly beautiful. It must have been all of 120 centimetres high and 90 centimetres across. And it was a mass of uncommonly fragrant yellow flowers, which on sunny days literally swarmed with every type of hoverfly and bee. It was sensational. At that point, we began to think that we needed to change our views on what classifies a weed. Technically, the majority of gardeners would regard oilseed rape as a weed, something agricultural, but we experienced the opposite. Our episode with oilseed rape was wholly positive. It was colourful, attractive, scented, wildlife friendly, and it became a talking point for visitors. A perfect plant indeed.

⊛⊛⊛

The old "wildlife" pond we had bought when first reclaiming the garden had become brittle and past its useful life. It was also clogged and overgrown. Therefore, we decided that it would be an improvement to have two ponds because of water's importance in the garden.

In a flash of inspiration, Evelyn suggested turning that old area of the pond into a beach area, complete with a rock pool feature. We bought a small round pond that was about 75 centimetres in diameter and about 45 centimetres deep. We removed the old pond and dug the area over, all the while fighting the roots of a very stubborn lilac tree, before levelling it off as we finished. We sank the pond into the centre of the site and covered the area with weed proof membrane. On top of that went bags and bags and bags of pea shingle with larger pebbles artistically placed to give a pleasingly natural effect.

The second area of water would be a "mountain stream" that issued forth from beneath the terrace. To accomplish this, we dug out the bed that ran from the entrance to the terrace and ran parallel to the path. When digging the hole to receive the pond we threw the spoil back up towards the terrace and created the slope for the stream and waterfall. We purchased for the project; the pond itself, which was about 120 centimetres by 90 centimetres; the stream with a reservoir at its head. This came cut price from a well-known Internet auction site. And a pump from a local garden centre. When it was finished it felt like a job well done but it didn't look like a mountain stream. At that point, circumstances smiled on us again. Some friends were moving house and had loads of free stone if we collected it. Not ones to look a gift horse in the mouth, we transported literally hundredweights of stone from Huntshaw to Bideford in our poor little bulgy tired trailer. After much huffing, puffing and backbreaking effort the finished result was satisfying and realistic.

❀ ❀ ❀

I eventually went into full-time employment with Royal Mail as a manager. This meant that I never had as much time for the garden as I would have liked. Consequently, it was always a little loose at the seams and never very tidy. This was something of a revelation to me because, over time, I began to notice the wildlife that used the garden preferred it that way. Slowly my awareness of the subject grew. Although I have always enjoyed wildlife, my interest was now changing from passive observation to an active desire to be involved.

Sometime later, my life took a turn for the better (or worse depending on your viewpoint, but I thought it a positive event) when Royal Mail made me redundant. The new board of directors under Alan Leighton (ex-director or something of the Asda supermarket chain) decided to get rid of 8000 managers. I was one of them. How I rejoiced. I received a little pension; just enough to get by on if one cut the cloth to fit the suit.

Freedom! This gave me more time to spend in the garden. To increase my knowledge in practical ways I invested in some gardening courses. The first course was garden design, the second was wildlife gardening, and the third was to the level of the Royal Horticultural Society certificate, level 2 as it was then. As I worked away at these courses and the garden, I felt myself leaning strongly towards the wildlife side of things.

❀ ❀ ❀

The summer of 2006 found us developing an interest in the National Garden Scheme and visiting numerous gardens to get ideas for our own little plot. Whilst looking through the "Yellow Book" we came across an East Devon garden that was described as wildlife friendly. Intrigued by this description and coupled with our own interest in wildlife we made plans to visit. It was Spilliford Wildlife Garden at Lower Washford, near Tiverton. It was owned by Dr Gavin Haig, who was quite a character.

The garden was a revelation. It extended to four acres and to the layman's eyes appeared unkempt, and uncared for. But that was before close analysis of the site. He took us on a guided tour and we could see that every part of the garden had been created as interrelated habitats and environments for wildlife. It catered for the lowest strata of the food chain to the highest, from insects and invertebrates to birds and mammals. It was a total contrast to the usual concept of gardening, which is neatness and tidiness. This garden had an extra dimension. It wasn't just about flora, just about flowers and shrubs and trees. It included fauna as well; it included activity and movement, and life. To use a modern management axiom, wildlife gardening gives you added value, and that gave me food for thought.

Somehow, the environment and the rest of creation often appear separate from us. It's something we watch on television, one or two steps removed from us. Through no fault of our own, because it's the way we're brought up and the culture that we're born into, the majority of us have the attitude that we live in an isolated bubble. We're happy as long as we can do what we want, have what we want, when we want it, and as long as nothing disrupts our cosy existence. Unfortunately, because of that situation, we've become disconnected from the real world. The planet's wildlife finds itself at breaking point because of mankind's thoughtlessness and greed.

Obviously, the man in the street cannot do much on an international scale, but he can do it in his own garden, and if others copied and did it in their own gardens, then those gardens make up a street. One street joins another street, and then joins to yet another street. These streets make up districts, and one district joins another district. And these districts make towns. Can you see where we're going with this? If we all became wildlife gardeners, even in the smallest courtyard garden, how green and pleasant our towns and cities would become. So how much more fulfilling our lives would be as a result, just by reconnecting with nature. As you can see, by now, I was truly smitten by the wildlife gardening bug.

This increased my desire to open for the National Garden Scheme. It also gave me the genesis of a plan that would make my garden appealing to them and at the same time champion the cause of wildlife gardening. I would follow the principles of this large East Devon garden but distil them down into what could be done for wildlife in a middling town garden. This would be our unique selling point, to use another modern management cliché. Our garden would be an educational garden. It would instruct and inform. It would help people to see that we can lend a hand to our pressurised wildlife, even in town. The idea being that although one garden isn't much in itself, if many gardens supported wildlife gardening principles, then as far as the wildlife is concerned those gardens take on the characteristics of one large garden; the sum of the total being more significant than the individual parts.

As events turned out, shortly after this visit, I contracted cellulitis in both my feet and was incapacitated for nearly two months, the problem being difficult to cure. Whilst being forced to put my feet up, I thought deeply about my project and slowly formulated plans to make it a reality. Although what the timescale for making it happen might be, was anybody's guess.

❀❀❀

By the new year of 2007, my illness had played itself out, and I was gently thinking about ways to make my plans become a reality. Then out of the blue, events took an unexpected leap forward. I regularly received an email newsletter from the television programme, "Gardener's World," and it discussed all things horticultural. But, January's newsletter was different. Besides the regular content, it laid down the challenge. *'Is your garden good enough to open for the public?'* It continued. *'Do you think your garden has what it takes to be on TV?'*

This fired my curiosity even more and further reading revealed that it was to be made by the independent producers "SixEight" for the television programme "Open Gardens." Each programme would follow two gardens as they worked to prepare themselves for assessment to be accepted into the National Garden Scheme. One would be successful; one would not. The unsuccessful garden owners would work through the summer to reach the required standard by the end of the season, and then be reassessed, and hopefully accepted.

The series would be fronted by the gardening personalities Carol Klein and Joe Swift. They would visit the gardens they were assigned to and would interview the garden owners and National Garden Scheme assessor. Through the season, Carol and Joe would encourage and support the garden owners as they progressed to the final assessment.

It all sounded rather interesting and so I responded, not knowing what to expect.

CHAPTER THREE

FEBRUARY

Our gardening life took a strange turn at the beginning of February; it became a flurry of emails. On the 4th, I responded to the "Gardener's World" email newsletter with an eight-word enquiry. I simply asked for more information. The following morning, I received an email reply from Gary Churchman, the series producer.

'Dear Henry

Thank you for responding to our item. As mentioned in the piece, we are making a television show for the second channel of our public service television broadcasting company presented by Carol Klein and Joe Swift. If you are unaware the show presents two gardens/gardeners who are both assessed by a National Garden Scheme County Organizer. One garden is accepted to show that summer and the other is told that it can't show that summer but will be reassessed for the following summer. We then follow the gardens/gardeners journey towards, in the one case, the open day and the re-assessment for the other. Carol Klein or Joe Swift are on hand to offer help and advice to those gardeners who wish it.

We are looking for gardens that can take part in the show and we are filming in Devon - if possible, we'd love to chat to you and possibly pop round for a visit to assess your suitability.

All the best

Gary.'

I thought it was time to approach Evelyn about this and tentatively mentioned it to her as we enjoyed our lunch. Evelyn, as is her way with most things, was cautious and not overly keen. She somehow sees all the difficulties and hard work involved with a project rather the fun, challenge, and end result of such an endeavour. However, by teatime I had, by gentle persuasion and hyping up the publicity for wildlife gardening, eventually talked her round. So she agreed. Later that evening another email was winging its way across cyber-space to the SixEight production company.

'Dear Gary,

Thanks for the quick response. I would look forward to being assessed for the programme if you want to. What I am aiming to do is to focus on demonstrating that a town garden can be made into a flourishing wildlife garden. Wildlife gardens don't have to be huge to be effective; the urban environment is now becoming even more important as a wildlife resource. Therefore, the garden will be educational too, not just 'pretty'. The idea is to encourage those who want to be wildlife gardeners but only have town gardens.

I look forward to hearing from you.

Kindest Regards

Henry'

Three minutes later, via this twenty-first century electronic postcard, I received a reply.

'Dear Henry,

Would it be possible to get your telephone number so that one of the team could give you a call for a quick chat?

All the best

Gary.'

The next morning, the 5th, when I opened my emails, my inbox contained a message from Belinda Knossos.

'Dear Henry

I work on the Open Gardens programme. Gary Churchman (Series Producer) passed on your email to me, and I wondered if you could please give me your phone number so that we can talk through your garden and I can explain some more about the programme…

Look forward to hearing from you.

Best wishes

Belinda Knossos'

The email contained her contact phone number. I sent her an email by return giving her mine and arranged to phone her the next day. This I did and she confirmed what Gary had mentioned in his email regarding who the face to camera presenter was to be. She established that our garden would have the pleasure of Carol Klein and went on to explain that there would be five filming days, each session taking about four hours. Belinda highlighted that the underlying atmosphere of the programme would be one of "jeopardy." A will they-won't they be successful approach would be employed to heighten the suspense of the situation. Later that afternoon another email was nested in my inbox.

'Dear Henry,

It was good to talk with you earlier today.

Please find attached the Open Gardens questionnaire - if you can fill it in and email it back that'll be great.

We will arrange to come and do a recce with a small handheld camera at some point next week. I will call and arrange this tomorrow.

Best Wishes

Belinda Knossos.'

The questionnaire followed the usual interrogation style. It asked questions about my partner, my garden, and me. It asked why I wanted to go into the "Yellow Book" and presented a variety of questions that revolved around preparations for opening and what it would mean to me to qualify for acceptance by the National Garden Scheme. Finally, it asked if I had taken part in any other television programmes before. I completed it that evening and emailed it back the following day.

Later that morning Belinda was back in contact with another email.

'Dear Henry,

Are you available for a recce on Wednesday 14th Feb at 10.30am? My colleague George Jefferies will be coming.

Please let me know ASAP.

Best wishes

Belinda.'

I emailed back confirming that the time was fine and giving directions so that George wouldn't get lost. I felt that I needed to do this because although we live in town, the layout of our road numbering is confusing, even to the locals. Even to the people who live in the road! At first glance, the numbering appears random, but there is some obscene logic to it, obviously worked out by a committee on the local council.

It is supposed to run from one to eighty-seven, and in some perverse way, it does, but its route is circuitous and torturous. It starts in Torrington Lane, a road that incidentally is not Sentry Corner. The numbering follows a right turn at the junction into Sentry Corner and along the road to a mini roundabout. Here it crosses over, doubles back on the opposite side of the road, and runs back into the road that isn't really Sentry Corner. Turning right, it follows a large loop keeping to the right hand side of the road until the mini roundabout eventually appears again. Going across this intersection or four-cross way as they call it in Devon, Sentry Corner carries on for another five houses, where, at the junction with Avon Road, it again crosses the road and doubles back to the mini roundabout. Going straight over that infernal mini roundabout the numbering goes on leading back up the opposite side of the street until it reaches the main road again. At this juncture the numbering turns right into the main road, a road of course that isn't Sentry Corner but now Gammaton Road on one side and Barton Tors on the other! Sentry Corner then carries on along this stretch of road for eight houses until it stops and becomes Barton Tors. How anyone could find us and visit, goodness only knows.

❀ ❀ ❀

It was now Friday the 8th. After that tentative enquiry on Tuesday, four days later Cherry Trees Wildlife Garden now had the possibility of being filmed for television.

It was a sobering thought. On reflection, Evelyn and I realised that after being carried along in the excitement, we had put ourselves under some pressure. We had wanted to open for the

National Garden Scheme at some point but now this had the effect of focusing our minds enormously.

A stroll around the garden with an eye to "the camera" was scary. The garden was by no means ready. At this time of year, what would we have to show a man who dealt in visual interest? The world looks strangely different when concentrating on little sections of the garden. Usually, there are so many distractions that the eyes aren't focused fully on individual things. It's not until one stops and closely observes what is actually in the garden that the panic sets in. It is a wonderful way to focus the mind.

We humans have wonderfully selective vision, the mind filters out what it doesn't want to see. What we manage to overlook is what most of the time is an eyesore. Bits of wood, old pots, canes, brickbats, and generally useless items clutter the garden and we never notice it. We had to clear it, and fast. We became ruthless, throwing away anything that we didn't need, was broken, or worn out.

To begin with, we cleared the shrubbery of "weeds" (unaware that sometime later we would plant so called weeds in there.) We kept focused on the wildlife aspect of course by trying to retain wildlife friendly things. It was a wet week, and for the next few days, we would get a daily soaking. We didn't mind though because we gained a remarkable feeling of accomplishment.

From the shrubbery, we worked down the garden towards the summerhouse, which these days we affectionately call "the doghouse" due to the way that one of our old dogs, Titch (a cute wheaten cairn terrier,) used to enjoy keeping himself out of the rain in the little kennel we had there.

Directly in front of the doghouse, there is a small bed bounded by an escallonia hedge. Old bits of board prevented the dogs going round the back of the Doghouse but they were unsightly. We removed them and replaced them with an old section of trellis we had lying around. A plastic compost bin, the type supplied by the local council, was tucked in the corner. We took the opportunity to remove that too. The result was surprising. It opened up the space and made it lighter and brighter.

Finally, we cleaned and tidied the greenhouse because, like most gardeners, we had used it as a storeroom during the winter. We filled it with pots, seed trays, watering cans, bamboo canes, wrapped up dahlias and fuchsias, besides the dead peppers and cucumbers we hadn't got around to clearing out yet. It took the two of us a whole day to complete.

❀ ❀ ❀

The morning of the 14th came upon us like an incoming tide. I had received a phone call the previous day informing me that my interview would be rather earlier than the 10.30 a.m. we had previously arranged. George Jefferies and his camera were due to arrive at 9.00 a.m. but, due to traffic on Dartmoor, he didn't arrive until 9.40.

I was unsure of what to expect but George turned out to be a bright young man with a designer beard and a ready smile. He was polite, well mannered, and extremely personable. He explained that he was an assistant producer and Carol Klein would be the expert assigned to present the garden to camera. He worked hard, putting me at ease by explaining how informal and easy going the interview was going to be and describing the camera and how to behave in front of it. I was surprised with the size of the camera. In her email, Belinda Knossos had said George would do the recce with a small handheld camera, but this was not what I would call small. I was expecting something like a digital movie camera but this monster appeared to be about seventy-five centimetres long, thirty centimetres deep, the same wide, and judging by the way he carried it from the car, pretty heavy.

After ten minutes or so, George asked me to show him round the garden. When we stepped out of the front door and into the cold front garden, I asked him how he wanted to handle it; nonchalantly he suggested I give him a guided tour. This threw me; I hadn't prepared to give an extemporaneous talk about the garden. I asked him what he wanted to know. In his calm courteous way, George recommended I lead him through each section of the garden, describing it, and any features it contained. He advised me not to look straight into the camera but slightly off to the side and up a bit. In effect, it meant that I had to talk to the top of his head!

Therefore, I did exactly that. I talked to the top of his head as the guided tour flowed like a river from the front garden, along the drive, through the beach area, across the lawn, under the ivy arch (where we paused for me to excitedly extol the virtues of this valuable plant) and along the apple and pear tree avenue to the greenhouse and doghouse. George and I continued onto the prospective summer wildflower meadow, back via the cottage garden border and into the faux Victorian walled vegetable garden with its resident hens, Phyllis and Mary. Sweeping out from there and back up the garden path, we came to the mountain stream and the shrubbery. Finally, we arrived at the terrace. I refuse to call it by the more common term, patio, because that horrid name, patio, came back from Spain with the package tourists of the 1980s. Let's get it straight. Britain is not Spain. The notion of the patio evokes baking sun, deckchairs, knotted handkerchiefs, lobster red faces and bodies, corned beef legs, and trousers rolled up to the knees. We do not get Spanish summers in this country, or if we do, they are as rare as hen's teeth. And I should know because as you are aware our garden contains two of them and there isn't a hen's tooth in sight. Therefore, in this garden, terrace it is, and terrace it will remain.

Back indoors; we sat in the living room and warmed up with a cup of coffee. George set the camera on a tripod, and for the next half hour, we filmed a short informal interview. This was in essence to find out more about me, to investigate my gardening ethos, and to examine what plans were due to be executed in the near future. He explained that one of the highlights of the programme is that Carol Klein did not merely present the programme but was also there to assist or advise the garden owner in ways to improve their garden. What did I want Carol to do? I didn't know; I hadn't given it any thought. I muttered something about improving the appearance of the driveway to make it more attractive to visitors.

That ended the interview. George packed up his camera and tripod, said his goodbyes and explained I would probably be hearing from SixEight in a couple of weeks. At the front door, we shook hands in farewell, and all the while, his smile had never left his face. As he lumbered back to his car under the weight of the filming equipment I couldn't help reflecting that he looked like a Nepalese Sherpa ready to conquer Everest, or a native bearer ready to cross darkest Africa and discover new horizons.

After I returned indoors, I went to the kitchen and asked Evelyn how she thought it went. She replied that it was 'all right,' and that I had 'made a decent fist of it.' That's one thing about these Devonian girls; they tell it as it is. You'll get no flattery from them. And another thing, don't ever expect one to get thrilled about anything. You may jump around blathering and waving your arms about shouting excitedly and pointing to a new insect you've discovered, and they'll just say, 'Oh, that's nice.' Let's get one thing straight though; this is by no means a criticism, just an observation; but then I've got to say that haven't I?

❈❈❈

While we waited for the verdict from SixEight, Evelyn and I decided to freshen up the garden a little, hopefully to make it attractive to the National Garden Scheme organiser. In keeping with the kind of garden we were creating, this included installing a sparrow terrace on the roof eves by the second bedroom window. Because of my size, (I could by no stretch of the imagination be called sylph-like) the use of a ladder was out of the question. It would have been too dangerous; one centimetre off the perpendicular and that would have been that. Not only would I have destroyed myself, I would have destroyed whatever I landed on. Twenty-five stone can make quite an impressive hole, and I had no desire to be the twenty-five stone that made it!

In the end, we decided that I should get out of the bedroom window, onto the flat roof of the extension, and then use a small pair of steps to access the eves to put up the nesting box. Simple. No it wasn't. It was anything but simple.

To begin with, I had to get out of the window. This window pivoted at the top thereby swinging upwards and outwards. It involved climbing up one pair of kitchen steps, straddling the windowsill, cocking the trailing leg up and over, then with my back on the windowsill sliding my body under the opened window and onto the flat roof. The problem with this was again my twenty-five stone bulk. It was a tight fit. I had to press my stomach in and "feed" it under the window, as though feeding a sheet through a mangle (which is also what it felt like.) Fifteen minutes later, I was outside and feeling relieved. Another fifteen minutes and the nest box was fixed up and awaiting new tenants.

The next challenge was to get back in. Now it could be thought that this would be easy enough, just the reverse of getting out. This wasn't the case though because I had to return my bulk back through, against the opening of the window. When I came out of the window, I came feet first, but I couldn't feed myself back through the window as I had come out, as though I were performing a "Fosbury Flop." I had to enter the window face down and force my belly over the sill. It hurt.

Evelyn had an idea that involved putting numerous pillows under my abdomen, now bruised and sore from the struggle against the window furniture. Duly padded, I forced myself forwards. Instantly I became wedged. Another endless amount of time was spent un-wedging me by wiggling me about and slowly removing some of the pillows. Little by little, I squeezed my bulk in through the window until there was more of me inside the house than out. I grabbed the inner windowsill and heaved myself in. I felt like a walrus hauling itself onto the beach. Something gave; I shot forward like a shell from a cannon and landed face down on the bed. Success! It had only taken just over half an hour to get back in. I was so exhausted I had to go and lie down for an hour. I rubbed smelly "Deep Heat" into my battered belly to relieve the pain. This incident isn't without irony; the window had been installed as a fire-escape window for a rapid evacuation.

The next job did risk injury. I had to trim the ten-foot high escallonia hedge by the compost bins and doghouse. Admittedly, it was a stepladder and not a long ladder, and Evelyn did hold the bottom of it, but it still felt like the north face of the Eiger. Whenever I go more than one foot off the ground I always feel top heavy with a centre of gravity that is un-naturally high, about three feet above my head as a rule.

Perched on top of this ladder I wielded an electric hedge-cutter with ungainly difficulty. After fifteen minutes, the weight of it, coupled with holding it at arm's length, made me feel somewhat rubbery. My arms sagged, my legs sagged, and the hedge sagged, so I promptly tipped head first into it. Fortunately, there was no permanent injury or damage done to either the hedge or me, even though it took me the best part of ten minutes to get myself out of it and ground myself again.

This episode encouraged me change my mode of attack. Rather than swaying around at height with a powered tool, I decided to use shears and extendable loppers. This leads me to another bitch. Don't try and cut any branch or twig more than the thickness of a cocktail stick with a cheap pair of shears bought from one these shopping "value houses" that have proliferated in recent years. As usual, it's false economy. I had gone no further than another two feet along the top of the hedge when a twig no wider than a person's little finger offered resistance to the shears. I applied what I would regard a reasonable amount of force for the job and instantly I felt my knuckles punch each other as the shear handles buckled. It hurt. The stupid things went straight into the trailer ready for a trip to the re-cycling centre. So, that is another salutary lesson. We only get what we pay for. One pricey item of good value is better than several cheaper ones of suspect quality. We never learn though do we? We always want non-existent bargains.

I eventually completed the task after many hours by pruning from ground level using the extendable lopper. It was one of those that can lengthen to about ten feet or more and once the cutting blades have been hooked with great difficulty around the target twig, is operated by pulling a length of cord. My arms ached, my back ached, and I had lost the will to live. Why does gardening always make some part of the body ache? Still, that's middle age for you.

❀ ❀ ❀

Attention now turned to the poor imitation of a Victorian vegetable garden. Two of the four plots had been given over to other uses. One was now occupied by a hen house, and the other was going to be an old-fashioned cornfield. Two miserly plots were left. Two plots of just twelve feet by five feet each. That's not much room for a crop rotation. What was I to do with them?

In the end, I settled on creating a raised bed system. This technique is perfect for the small garden, and ideal for organic methods. Firstly, it eliminates the need for heavy digging (anything to save a person's back has got to be a good thing.) Secondly, it reduces the amount of weeding that needs to be done (because plants are grown so close together they act as ground cover, starving the weeds of light.) And finally, it keeps the soil structure in good condition (because it is never walked on.)

After measuring up, and being suitably shocked at how much wood was needed, it was off to the builder's merchant timber yard with the trailer. I returned with over thirty-three metres of fifteen centimetres wide gravel board and over sixteen metres of five centimetres by five centimetres carcassing. From these basic ingredients I fashioned seven two metres by sixty centimetres raised beds. I even managed to come across two wooden finials in the shed, so I put them on the inside corners of the two beds nearest the path. The effect was delightful. It was an epic job. Thank goodness for electric saws, electric drills, and powered screwdrivers. Although I must admit that at this stage, the beds had the appearance of a row of empty graves in a cemetery.

Before filling in the beds, I dug over each one in turn to make sure there was no impermeable pan to prevent good drainage. This is one of the advantages of the raised bed system, good drainage. I also made sure there were no deep-rooted perennial weeds skulking in the depths ready to spring surprises on me. Although I must say, contrary to what all the textbooks and how to books say, it is physically impossible to clear every vestige of these cunning characters. But the positive from the exercise is that, yes, they will come back, but at a rate and number that can be tackled with ease. As each perennial weed pops up above the soil to have a look around, you can pretend to be a true Tudor and like Henry the Eighth, chop its head off. It stands to reason that proper preparation is essential, but we don't want to become neurotic about it.

Rubbery trugs must be one of the best inventions for gardeners in years. They are not the prettiest containers in the world but they are superb for holding prunings, grass cuttings, water (except those trugs designed not to hold water) and for carrying compost and soil. Rather than filling the wheelbarrow with compost, I filled the trugs with compost and transported them to the vegetable garden. Once there, rather than fighting the wheelbarrow up the steps and turning it in a tight space, it was a simple case of lifting the trug and tipping its contents over the wall and onto the beds.

The addition of some topsoil rounded it off. After digging it in, mixing it well, and levelling it off, the job was almost finished. The laying of chipped bark on the paths between the beds completed the job and it looked a treat. There's something about the appearance of open, clean, fresh looking soil. Having said that, bare soil is not the ideal for organic gardening, or wildlife gardening for that matter, because bare soil allows the nutrients to wash away and weed growth to proliferate. But still, it wouldn't be like that for long, I had grandiose plans for those seven raised beds.

❀❀❀

On the 23rd, I read correspondence on the letters page of The Times newspaper challenging the value of ivy, and I couldn't resist responding to it. In doing so, I became one of those smug little oiks who can boast that they have had a letter published in The Times. Thus, an enjoyable string of letters followed that lasted into the second week of March. The names of the correspondents have been redacted for obvious reasons.

23rd February: Growing problem.

Sir, Does anyone else share my concern for the way our countryside is being taken over by ivy?

It seems wherever I am in East Anglia there it is. Growing in all the hedgerows, climbing over walls and up trees, breaking off branches and pulling trees over in the wind, shutting out the light and covering everything in dark green, all year round.

Is there anything that can be done, or that should be done, to resist the relentless march of this strangling growth?
X. X. Xxxxxxx, Barningham, Suffolk.

26th February: In defence of ivy.

Sir, May I, as a wildlife horticulturalist, spring to the defence of the ivy?

Nothing should be done to it. With our wildlife under the relentless pressure of environmental degradation, ivy is a lifesaver. It provides food, shelter, and breeding spaces for birds, bees, butterflies, and many other insects. There is in fact no better plant for wildlife.

It does not damage walls that are in good condition; rather it protects them from the extremes of the British weather. Neither does it strangle trees or pull them down; any tree that does come down would have fallen anyway because of disease or death. Occasionally a limb or even a tree may come down in gale force winds but that is hardly the ivy's fault.

So, rather than condemn ivy through what is often received wisdom, let's enjoy it. Without it, our wildlife would be impoverished and so would our quality of life.
Henry Butterfield (that's me!) Bideford, Devon.

26th February:

Sir, X. X. Xxxxxxx is in distinguished company when he complains about the way our countryside is being taken over by ivy.

Queen Mary, widow of George V, spent the years of the Second World War with her niece, the Duchess of Beaufort, at Badminton House in Gloucestershire. During her stay, she spent many determined hours organising raiding parties of estate workers to seek out the dreaded green stuff and destroy it where it grew.

Perhaps the Prince of Wales can be persuaded to follow in his great-grandmother's footsteps.

Xxxx Xxxxxxx, London SW11.

27th February: Ivy League.

Sir, Contrary to belief, ivy is not a parasite of trees. It is shallow rooted and does not compete with its host for water, except perhaps with shallow-rooted trees in drought.
Xxxx Xxxxxxxxxx, The Woodland Trust.

27th February:

Sir, Ivy holds old walls together, pulls down dead tree branches during gales - thus letting in light - and is, with holly, an intrinsic part of a Christmas carol.
Xxx Xxxxx, Brecon.

27th February:

Sir, It used to be said that lawyers' mistakes were hanged, doctors' mistakes were buried and architects' mistakes were covered in ivy.

Looking at our city centres, one can only wish for a fast-growing variety that has a taste for concrete and a head for heights. Xxxxxx Xxxx, London SW13.

28th February: Ivy the terrible.

Sir, The thoroughly negative reputation of ivy is, I fear, too well rooted in English history in spite of Mr Butterfield's valiant attempt to rescue it.

In 1611, the Countess of Oxford, widow of Edward de Vere and a former maid of honour to Queen Elizabeth, was having a trying time with her son, Henry, the 18th Earl of Oxford. At the age of 17 he had fallen into the wayward company of his first cousin, John Hunt, who was not only running up huge debts in the young Earl's name but was also encouraging him to neglect his duties as an esquire to King James.

In exasperation, Countess Elizabeth wrote to her late husband's brother-in-law by his first marriage, Sir Robert Cecil, beseeching the Secretary of State to discipline Hunt. The letter reads, in part: "[I] am therefore absolutely resolved, unless I shall presently obtain the absolute banishment of him and his confederates from my son... for the world will never believe (except I make it known by a public renouncing of his further government) but I might with suit unto his great and powerful allies and friends have easily procured this ivy to be plucked away from this young oak whose growth is so much hindered by it."
Xxxxxx Xxxx, Newcastle-under-Lyme, Staffs.

3rd March: Creeping danger.

Sir, With reference to the ivy debate, Prospero, in The Tempest, warned us about the perfidiousness of ivy when referring to his brother:
"That now he was
The ivy which had hid my princely trunk,
And suck'd my verdure out on't."

Xxxxxxxxx Xxxxx-Xxxxxxxx, Carmel, California.

6th March: The scarlet ivy.

Sir, The debate about ivy and references to it has been too insular so far.

Ivy as a destroyer of trees and walls, which had appeared in Pliny, was commonplace all over Europe in the renaissance, for instance as a metaphor for a whore. But it was entangled too with the symbolism of the elm-embracing vine, as an image of mutual and fruitful love. Both traditions go back at least to the poets of Rome, in particular Catullus. This correspondence should surely not cease but spread.

Xxxxxx Xxxxx, Emeritus Professor of Spanish, Trinity College, Dublin.

10th March: True grip.

Sir, If this correspondence should not cease but spread we should note that it was not only in the Renaissance and by the poets of ancient Rome that the ivy "was entangled... with the symbolism of the elm-embracing vine, as an image of mutual and fruitful love" (ibid). In the music hall song by A. J. Mills and Harry Castling we have:

"Just watch the ivy, on the old garden wall,
Clinging so tightly whate'er may befall.
As you grow older I'll be constant and true:
Just like the ivy, I'll cling to you.

The song was no doubt inspired in part by Cowper's lines:
"As creeping ivy clings to wood or stone,
And hides the ruin that it feeds upon."

Xxxx Xxxxxx, Cinderford, Gloucestershire.

That was the end of the correspondence. It didn't spread; it ceased after this letter!

✿ ✿ ✿

During the last week of the month, I received phone calls from both SixEight and the National Garden Scheme assistant county organiser, Jo Hynes.

SixEight informed me that we were to be included in the sixty gardens shown on the programme, and that our five filming days would be in March, April, May, July, and August (where June went I don't know.) Each session would take around half a day to film. Some sessions would be filmed in the morning, some in the afternoon. The first session would start at 8.00 a.m. on the 22nd of March.

Jo Hynes phoned and asked if we could meet in advance of the filming so that she could go over a few things with me and have a look around the garden. She needed to formulate some idea of what she was going to comment on and what areas of the garden needed improvement. SixEight had no idea we were having this clandestine meeting. As far as they were concerned, the first time I would meet Jo would be on the first day's filming. Jo highlighted that the series producers would focus on the jeopardy aspect of applying to join the National Garden Scheme. I remembered that Belinda Knossos from SixEight had stressed that point earlier in the month.

It's all about making exciting television I suppose. This series would be hyping up the relaxing and enjoyable act of gardening to the level of a job interview, or taking an exam. And as I was to discover as the months went by, actions and events that are seen on screen are not necessarily what they appear, as we shall see later.

✹✹✹

So, February came to a close. When the month began my gardening life was calm and relaxing, but now, there was a busy summer ahead. Would Cherry Trees' puny little garden be acceptable for the National Garden Scheme? Would they accept a small town garden that was not only in the process of development but consisted of rotting logs, untidy corners, and deliberately grown "weeds?" Other gardeners would have much more acceptable gardens, gardens of rolling acres, vast beds of interesting plants and multitudes of exotic features. It struck me that this could all turn out to be extremely embarrassing, but it was too late to turn back now. We had to face March, and what a March it turned out to be.

CHAPTER FOUR

MARCH

At the start of the month, a walk around the garden with a notebook informed me that there were a number of unfinished jobs that urgently required attention, especially if Jo Hynes and a film crew were coming to visit. One job in particular caught my eye. For more than fifteen years the gutter on the bottom shed had waited for an end piece and a downspout. For far too long the rain poured out of the gutter and whirled wildly into space, landing in the water butt as and how it may. Annoying little things like this needed be addressed.

Therefore, I engaged in that unwise practice of visiting places such as B&Q, Jewsons and St John's Garden Centre (thank goodness for accounts, loyalty cards and discounts.) Impulse plays an important part in my garden shopping, as I'm sure it does with the majority of us, and an afternoon out with the car and trailer saw me arrive home with a marvellous array of objects. These included; two pots of Muscari, a well grown rosemary plant, one hundred and fifty litres of general-purpose compost, two log rolls, four metres of turf, twelve forty-five by forty-five centimetre square buff paving slabs, a new pond pump (half price in a sale), four bags of grey shingle for the vegetable garden, a short length of gutter, two down spouts, and two gutter ends. (You can pause and catch your breath after that sentence if you like.)

To continue; I also wanted some five centimetres by two and a half centimetre batten for a little picket fence I decided to make for the mini summer wildflower meadow, so I finally arrived home with thirty-two metres of it. Don't ask me why, but it only came in a pack of eight, four metre lengths. As it turned out, I needed every centimetre of it. I made one last journey to collect five large bags of horse manure from Evelyn's granddaughter, Kayleigh. It was decent, good quality, straw based manure, not this low quality stuff that uses sawdust instead. The compost heap and the base of the runner beans would benefit greatly from this beneficent gift.

A busy time was spent making the little picket fence (it took me over four hours to cut the uprights into forty-five centimetre lengths with pointy ends) and assembled it around the prospective summer wildflower meadow. A long, cold, day, meant a salty drip never ceased to be far from the tip of my nose. Meanwhile, Evelyn attacked the path that ran beside the apple and pear trees. She laid the twelve slabs from the archway to the greenhouse in one day. Superb work! We awaited the North Devon NGS organiser's visit.

❀ ❀ ❀

At 2.00 pm precisely Jo Hynes' maroon coloured Range Rover pulled up outside. Getting out of it I could see her foaming head of long salt and pepper hair and bright intelligent smile. It made her most becoming. She wore a highly patterned cross banded jumper with ethnic style jacket, black denim jeans, and stout working shoes.

Her promptness indicated that she was a well-organised person, which was proved immediately. We made our introductions, discussed a little about the NGS and the way it was involved with the Open Gardens programme, then in no time at all, we went out in the garden discussing the venture.

It didn't start well. The colossal pile of tree prunings that were piled on top of a heap of topsoil s came into view as we strolled along the driveway.

'What's all this?' She asked

'Ah, now that's a few trimmings I'm going to dispose of shortly. And the soil's going to be spread around the garden shortly as well.'

'Umm.'

I am ashamed to say that this topsoil had been hanging around for two and a half years. It came from a friend's garden after he dug out a bank at the rear of his house to make space for a car. I couldn't bear the thought if it going to the re-cycling centre and ending up as landfill, so I offered to take it away and use it in our garden. We thought it might come in useful, but it turned into another of those jobs that we hadn't got around to.

As we crossed the lawn Jo couldn't help but notice the bare stringy patches of earth that the hen's scratching created during the wet weather.

'Is this supposed to be the lawn?' she queried.

'Ah, yes.' I began the explanation. 'We placed the ark there whilst moving the hen house from the site of the new wildflower meadow and into the vegetable garden.'

'Are you going to fix it in time?'

It was my turn to say 'Umm.'

The damage a pair of hens can wreak in a few days is immense. Scratch, scratch, scratch, all the time, they could compete with pigs for ground clearance.

We wandered along the apple and pear avenue and arrived at the greenhouse. Adjacent to it stood my pride and joy, a leaf mould bin. Wonderful stuff is leaf mould. It takes an eternity to break down but the result is a deep brown crumbly substance that helps give the soil a friable texture, and puts it in good heart. Jo did not seem impressed with the aesthetic appeal of bits of chicken wire, and the remains of an old camping toilet tent frame which held the wire together.

'What in Heaven's name is this?' she blurted

'That's a leaf mould bin.'

'Is it?'

'Umm.'

'It'll have to go.'

'Right." I glanced at her from the corner of my eye.

'You need to really tidy this area up.' And off she went like the Queen of Sheba with me following behind in her wake.

I'm afraid the rest of the prospective highlights of the garden were more like lowlights. The future summer wildflower meadow lay naked and barren as a crumpled brown sheet. The cottage garden border and the wheat field looked no better. As for the woodland edge bed, it was more like a shrubbery.

As we walked around and analysed the work that needed to be done it didn't take much intelligence to recognise that this garden would not be open to the public this year. Jo personified politeness and tact as she broke the news to me, although I sensed from the beginning that this would be her answer.

Back indoors, we enjoyed a cup of coffee as we warmed ourselves through. That half an hour in the garden was chilling even though we both wrapped up well. Still, we chatted away and got on well, Jo's sense of humour resonating with mine. Finally, we agreed that I would have to deal with the driveway before filming started and then my projects for the summer would be the leaf mould bin and the various beds

Two air kisses later, Jo was in her Range Rover and away back to Dolton, where she lived. In a fortnight's time, we would go the same procedure again, but this time in front of a camera.

❀❀❀

The following fortnight saw great activity. As before, a visit to B&Q and St John's Garden Centre saw me arriving home with yet more stuff. The list included (wait for it, wait for it); six rolls of turf (some half price because it was yellowing,) six buff paving slabs, a tray of six polyanthuses (£1,) some Cineria (25p,) two violet odorata, a pot of tete a tete daffodils, and two rolls of green plastic fencing (two metres long by half a metre high.)

In evidence during this period was the squeak, squeak, squeak, of the wheelbarrow wheel as I finally moved the soil from the driveway and distributed it around the garden beds, topping them up nicely. After a good sweeping and wash down, the reclaimed driveway looked respectable and presentable again.

Much of this impoverished soil made its way to the summer wildflower meadow. The soil here is much too fertile so we removed the top six inches or so and spread it around the garden beds. We left it to settle and let the rain leach out even more fertility.

Evelyn focused on repairing the lawn. Some of the soil from the driveway went on this as did a number of the turves. I used the rest of the turves to create another seating area behind the small hedge of conifers, which left one turf for Phyllis the hen's scratching treat. Carol Klein showed interested in this and we discussed it at a later filming session and therefore so shall we.

The 21st arrived, the morning before the first filming day. My *Petunia "Easy Wave"* plug plants arrived as well. What typical inconvenience. Why couldn't they be delivered one or two days later? (By the way, they're absolute rubbish as wildlife plants – don't buy them.) Evelyn and I did plan to purge the garden on a fanatical tidying spree. Although a wildlife garden can get away with being rather untidy around the seams it cannot get away with being an urban excuse for an unregistered recycling centre, especially if it's going to be appraised for the National Garden Scheme and appear on television.

The plug tray of seventy petunias was transferred to the potting shed for my first potting foray of the year. As I began to prepare for the potting the blessed potting bench collapsed. It had been used it for years, but being wooden in a damp environment it had rotted through. The slightest bit of weight and that was that. Fortunately, there was a galvanised potting bench in the greenhouse. Therefore, after clearing out the rotten and powdery wooden bench I replaced it with the good one. Potting was duly finished late morning.

That put us under increased pressure. There was so much to do. The roof of the hen house was a holding area for, what we considered useful, bits of timber. This required sorting out. Plant pots, seed trays, screen blocks, tools, piles of rubbish, and any number of other odds and sods lay strewn around the garden. All this needed to go somewhere, and much to my disgruntlement that somewhere ended up being my potting shed. Later that afternoon my potting shed resembled the black hole of Calcutta. It looked like the cupboard under the stairs where we put things when we cannot find anywhere else to put them. It became a horticultural black hole. It was bulging so much one could hardly shut the door, but with the persuasion of a shoulder and a foot it squeezed gently into place. Shooting the bolt and securing the padlock completed the job. Much sweeping followed until darkness prevented any more work. We ended the day exhausted, but, as far we could reckon, fully prepared for tomorrow.

❀ ❀ ❀

The 22nd arrived, filming day number one. At 8.00 am prompt, a silver grey Hyundai estate car pulled up outside the house and a feeling of apprehension gripped me. I wondered what these television types would be like. The car doors opened and out tumbled a total of five young men and women bubbling in good spirits. I recognised George Jefferies. Being an assistant producer, I thought he would be in control of the operation, and this proved to be the case.

Jo Hynes was not due to arrive until 9.30 so they asked me to show them round the garden highlighting all the interesting areas. As we did this they filmed various bits that caught their eye. It all seemed somewhat random. After the tour George said that he wanted to film me writing my book. My summerhouse come study is only eight feet by eight feet, so as you can imagine it did not leave a lot of room for the film crew and me. Therefore, I sat at my desk in front of my laptop while the crew squeezed tight into the doorway, tight like sardines in a tin, behind the cameraman. This cameraman was very skilled considering the space he had to work in. I felt a bit over dressed for this; there I was wearing my gardening coat and hat typing away at the keyboard. Normally, I would take my hat and coat off, turn on the halogen heater and settle down to write, all snug and cosy. To be honest, it gave the impression that it was all a bit rushed. It appeared that they wanted to get all these little odd bits filmed before Jo Hynes turned up.

Right on cue, Jo's Range Rover pulled up outside. She wandered up the driveway, smiling away in that charming way of hers, and was duly welcomed by the film crew. They introduced Jo to me as though we had never met. They of course, knew nothing of our secret meeting earlier in the month when we agreed the outcome in advance. I felt like a spy keeping it under wraps and not letting slip that we already knew each other. Anyway, regardless of that, we all hit it off straight away and immediately developed a good rapport with each other.

George organised us to begin the garden tour that, unbeknown to him, Jo and I had previously rehearsed. He reminded us to ignore the camera, relax, and be as conversational as we could. To get things in motion he asked me what the garden was like when we first moved in. As I am inclined to do, I thought I'd keep things light. I opened with a tall story.

'When we first moved in here, the garden was full of shillet. As you can see, we've used shillet alongside the drive, we've used shillet to make a sundial, and we even used shillet to make a cleaner.'

George furrowed his forehead and leaned towards me. 'What? Make a cleaner?' Even Jo looked at me querulously.

'Yea, it's quite simple. We found out accidentally that if we powdered it down to a fine dust and then mixed it with a binding lubricant such as cooking oil it became the perfect cleaning agent. It was brilliant for worktops. It's slightly abrasive action took out even the most stubborn stain. We're going to market it under the trade name of "Shillet Bang."'

George and Jo thought it all very ingenious, but then silence. Realisation slowly dawned. We enjoyed the laugh and George told me it couldn't be included in the edit because it would seem like a crafty way of product placement, which they aren't allowed to do.

As we passed the totally uninspiring slab of concrete that goes under the grand title of a driveway, there was an under the breath mutter of 'need to do something here' from Jo; and so we moved on.

Coming onto the lawn we walked straight towards the rotary washing line we forgot to remove. Why do we forget such obvious things like that? We removed all the minutiae but forgot this massive edifice.

Jo came at it straight out of the starting blocks. "And what species is this?"

I laughed and off the top of my head responded with, *'Tripodius Greenstringius.'* Muffled mirth came from the film crew.

'Presumably you can move this for open day?'

Knowing how tight that rotary line was wedged into the ground I jokingly replied, 'Yes, with a hacksaw.'

'With a hacksaw,' Jo repeated looking incredulous. Avoiding her gaze, I looked down and saw the grass was still bare from Phyllis the hen scratching it up when I moved her run. I waited for a comment, but thankfully none was forthcoming, just the stare of Medusa.

As we approached the greenhouse we came face to face with my leaf mould bin, that rustic looking beast of a thing. Tucked cosily next to the fence, the pile of beech and ash leaves were still rotting nicely within the wall of chicken wire, and old camping toilet frame that was originally destined for the re-cycling centre. On hind-sight, perhaps we should have let it go there in the first place. We agreed that this was a definite area for improvement. It was an eyesore.

Next stop was the summer wildflower meadow, or rather the plot with aspirations of being a summer wildflower meadow. There it was, the size of a sheet of hardboard, an inert oblong of blank brown soil apparently devoid of all life.

Jo spontaneously went into her spiel and threw me immediately onto the back foot. 'Plenty of potential there then?' she exclaimed.

'Yep, believe it or not it's going to be a summer wildflower meadow.'

She then bowled me the googly. 'Which kind of grassland are you going for? Are you going to go for chalk grassland or acid bog?'

My mind instantly went blank. This is the typical result of lack of preparation. As usual the old axiom was right, fail to prepare is to prepare to fail. I should have known she would ask me that question. So did I have an intelligent confident answer? No. I just came out with the pathetic and inarticulate response, 'general purpose.'

'General purpose?' Jo had sussed out that I was bluffing. 'So presumably this is to attract your butterflies and stuff?'

'Yes, that's the one, yes.'

Feeling duly humbled by my unpreparedness and feeling as though I had just made a 'der-brain' idiot of myself for national television, we headed for the vegetable garden.

As we opened the squeaky old rusty gate, we looked forward and to the left. In this vacant bed lay the old fashioned cornfield. Or again, what purported to be a cornfield, looking for all intents and purposes just another lifeless chocolate brown slab waiting for life to spring forth. I looked appealingly at Jo and uttered in a less than confident tone. 'This is going to be a cornfield.'

'This is going to be a cornfield?' Jo stared at me totally unconvinced.

That was the end of the conversation as far as the cornfield was concerned.

Adjacent to the cornfield lived Phyllis the hen in her modular henhouse. I am proud of that because I designed and built it myself. I think my modular design for the hen house is revolutionary. It comprises four walls; each wall a "stand alone" wall made of fifteen centimetres by fifteen centimetres timber carcassing and covered with chicken wire. One wall has a built in door for access and one end has space for roosting. Egg laying takes place in a plastic construction known as an "Eglu," manufactured by a company called Omlet. The walls then butt up against each other at the four corners and are then screwed together. The whole assembly can be dismantled, moved, and reassembled in the course of a morning. It could be recognised as a prefabricated building I guess.

Unfortunately, shortly before this filming day took place, I had two hens but Mary, the other one, had unknowingly become egg-bound and died. So that was another embarrassment.

What happened next could be misconstrued as bribery, although there was none intended. It was merely a gesture of goodwill. I introduced Jo to Phyllis and looked to see if she had lain that morning, and there lay one medium sized brown egg nestled in the straw. I collected it and gave it to Jo. Thus began one of the corniest conversations in history.

'There you are; one little egg.' I placed in her hand.

'Eggcellent, breakfast time,' she responded.

'Yes, she lays one of those every day.'

'Does she? What a good girl.'

'Yes she is, Eggcellent.'

As we left the vegetable garden, the cottage garden couldn't be missed. It looked sad. There were just a few plants breaking the barren plain of more naked soil. I must admit, there certainly wasn't much garden for Jo to see and the team to film. I felt something of a fraud to be honest.

When we got to the terrace the crew busied around and arranged us neatly. We sat next to each other at the table, just like Bill and Ben the flowerpot men. Jo and I discussed the project (as we agreed the other day behind the scenes).

Her opening comment was; 'Do you know; I've never been to look at a garden quite like this, in the terms, it's not a garden for people; it's a garden for wildlife.'

We discussed all the areas of the garden that she was concerned about. Finally we concluded that by the time Jo comes for the re-assessment in the late summer the jobs to be completed or rectified are: the cornfield, the meadow, the cottage garden, the front driveway, and the leaf mould bin, besides all the other jobs that need doing during the summer. No pressure there then!

It was time for the rejection. Jo gazed kindly at me and said, 'I think for this year, I'm going to say no. Thanks for offering but I don't think we can use your garden this year.'

I wasn't duly disappointed because I knew it was coming.

We had to go through the filming twice because the crew only had one camera. First they filmed Jo and her comments, and then turning to me, we went through it again to get my reactions.

We then spent time with the crew filming me in various ways of expressing regret at failure and comments that I shall be positive in my reaction. They settled with my inarticulate prattling statement… 'Well, yes, it is quite disappointing, but it was a reasonable comment that she made about the long term projects I've got to address. So, yes, it is disappointing, but it's a challenge and I look forward to it.'

The filming team seemed happy with that.

✹✹✹

The next day boxes of nicotiana, antirrhinum, and pelargonium plug plants arrived in the post. Time was precious so there was an immediate pressure to get them in the potting shed in readiness to put them in proper pots. You've guessed it. This necessitated taking everything out of the potting shed again.

I thought I would kill two birds with one stone. (That's not a good simile/cliché for a wildlife gardener I know, but I couldn't think of anything better.) So I decided to go through all my flower pots accumulated over the years. I picked out all the shapes, sizes, and colours I have never used but thought might come in handy sometime (does that sound familiar?) They were a jumble of large (about half a metre or more in diameter) to small (ten centimetres or less.) They had been stored badly so some of them were bent and misshapen, and some of them were split. They were a tasteless palette of colours too; black, brown, lavender, magenta, pink, and a ghastly assortment of other hues. I was glad to see the back of them.

Being the old fashioned and sentimental fellow that I am, I'm afraid that I did keep my terra cotta clay pots and saucers, even though I hardly ever use them. There is something nostalgic about clay pots. In this world of disposable plastic pots and trays they feel timeless. It's like a link to the past, to our forefathers, all heavily involved with the Victorian and Edwardian gardens and greenhouses. They are so tactile. They have a firm dry dusty texture, and earthy appearance; it makes them desirable, to me anyway. It took all day clearing and tidying and at day's end there were four compost sacks full of rubbish ready for the re-cycle centre.

❀❀❀

By the end of the month things had progressed well. March's sowing was complete. Broad beans and peas were snug in their toilet roll tubes, hanging basket sweet peas, tomatoes, and aubergines were cosy in their individual three inch pots. The garlic, onions, shallots, early potatoes, thyme and chives were in their positions and growing strongly. The cottage garden border received a broadcast sowing of a cottage garden seed mix.

We tackled the summer wildflower meadow. The naked brown plot of great potential was to be sown. It was prepared in the standard manner for all lawns, complete with that ridiculous way of firming the soil by marching up and down taking fairy steps while pushing your heels into the ground. The mix comprised of fourteen wild flower species, and five species of grass. The major flower species were; ox-eye daisy, red campion, ribwort plantain, self-heal, white campion and wild carrot. The grasses; browntop bent, crested dogstail, and three kinds of fescue. We thought it was a good balance and it would be interesting to see what actually came up.

The month ended. We stood and looked around the garden. All we've fully accomplished is the wildflower meadow, and only time will tell if it's successful. What will we have finished by the time the next filming session arrives? Would we be up to scratch?

CHAPTER FIVE

APRIL

April the 1st turned out to be a sick joke, and we were made to feel real April fools. That evening Evelyn and I were due to go to a 50th wedding anniversary party, but just before we were to leave there was carnage in the garden.

We called the dogs to come in, so that we could go out, but there was no response; a sure sign that they were up to mischief. Regrettably, in our rush to get ready, after feeding our dear solitary hen, we had carelessly left the hen house door unfastened. Losing her patience through the dogs lack of response, Evelyn went out to get them and stumbled upon a scene of pure horror. Phyllis had come out of her run and jumped the vegetable garden wall. The dogs, being Cairn terriers, immediately thought it was time for some sport and attacked her. To them it made no difference, be it a hen or a rat or a cat. A terrier's instinct is, if it moves quickly, get after it. She was barely alive and well short of feathers, she was in sore straights. With heavy hearts we gently put her back into the run and went to the party, undecided what to do with her. We hoped she might settle and gently recover.

When we got there I felt so deflated and joyless that I could not go into the gathering. Evelyn went in and associated with everyone, but I couldn't force myself out of the car. I just sat there for the whole evening and moped. However, on our return the decision had been made for us, because when we went to the henhouse Phyllis had died, probably of shock.

I felt distraught and sad. It's strange how we become attached to something like a hen. Although I guess it's more because of the violent way of her death as opposed to dying of old age. So, we were without a hen. The star of the first sequence of filming, the star of the show, was deceased, she was no more, she had shuffled off this mortal coil and gone to meet her maker, she had gone back to the ground from whence she came, she was an ex-hen, in short, she was dead. Hens were central to the appeal of our garden so there was nothing for it but to head out on a hen hunting hike and buy more.

Fortunately, it just so happened that a farmer's wife in Buckland Brewer bred chickens and she had some point of lay birds ready. As we went along the farm track we could see that she had a variety of birds, but we only wanted two. We made ourselves known and the owner took us to the shed. There were scores of birds following her as though they worshipped her.

'What d'you want?' she said.

'Not sure. What have you got?'

'All sorts. Take yer pick.'

We finally we settled on another warren, and a variety called a silver leg. It was a new hybrid, a white variety, with similar laying qualities as the warren. In contrast to Phyllis and Mary who were raging psychopaths, these were both extremely friendly and biddable, which was a bonus. Getting pecked every time your hens come near you can be rather disconcerting. Our dogs in particular had suffered from hairless snouts for some time.

Initially, in a poor imitation of the way Beverley Nichols named his cats, I called them "Three" and "Four" because they were the third and fourth hens we had owned. In no time, "Three" had settled in and laid an egg. Evelyn immediately renamed them. "Three" was now "April" because she started laying in April, and "Four" had become "May" because she would no doubt start laying in May, which she did. They were sold as point of lay, and point of lay they were.

❀❀❀

Meanwhile, time was rushing by at the speed of light. Well, not quite that fast, in reality not even at the speed of sound, but here it was, the 7th, and the next filming day was the 16th. I still had construction work to do in the prospective courtyard. During the week I ventured into the builder's merchants and brought home bags of sand, bags of cement, and concrete blocks in my little trailer, whose tyres looked fit burst under the weight. The stage was set for the construction of the courtyard trough. When planted up this was to inject a blaze of colour and to create a pleasing invitation to enter the garden.

It became a long and rugged day. I started at 9.00 am and made concrete block towers at each end of the courtyard wall to avoid the necessity of walking backwards and forward to where they were stored. I didn't have a cement mixer, so had to mix by hand. Piles of sand, bags of cement and buckets of water were duly, back-breakingly, turned into malleable mortar. I had learned my concrete mixing lessons.

It wasn't until I had started to lay out the blocks and lay down the mortar foundation that I realised the drop from one end to the other was considerable. From left to right, which was a fraction over two metres, it dropped dramatically by over half a concrete block's depth. I scurried around collecting bits of old block and brickbats to try and create some form of level. It looked quite peculiar when I had done, but hey, so what, it would be disguised under render when complete. When I had finally finished, the wall trough appeared reasonable enough to a non-builder type like me. I tidied up around the inspection cover and the crumbly bits of the courtyard by using the remaining concrete to fill holes and build up hollows so that the area looked reasonably level and complete.

My work day finished at 5.30 pm, but it had not been uneventful. I had pinched my fingers moving concrete blocks; hit my left index finger with a 5lb lump hammer, which resulted in an intense throb and a blue-black bruise, and in the end had an aching back from concrete mixing by hand. But, it had been rewarding.

❀❀❀

The pressure was beginning to build so I went to St Johns' Garden Centre to get four bags of top soil to fill the new trough garden. But, the usual thing happened. Besides buying the topsoil I came away with, three huge bags of potting compost, two large terra-cotta pots for the holly bushes (I saw a well-trained holly in a pot in the sales area), pea/bean mesh for growing legumes, Coolglass for shading the greenhouse, another roll of plastic fencing, two native primroses (I couldn't resist them), and a pack of twenty, eight centimetre square pots.

      Once home, I filled the trough with the four bags of top soil and three bags of compost. I mixed it all together. It was hard graft but it looked good. In the evening Evelyn painted the trough and the wall with 'Country Cottage Cream' masonry paint and made it look even better. We stood back and surveyed our work. Not bad at all we thought.

      The next few days were manic. Plants were coming thick and fast and the pressure of sowing and potting on seedlings was mounting by the minute. Trailing antirrhinum and trailing lobelia plugs arrived with the post, so they needed potting to bring on. This also applied to my home-sown *'Alicante'* tomatoes, aubergines, dwarf dahlias, and tagetes *'Lemon Gem'*. I grow tagetes in the greenhouse to keep whitefly off the tomatoes. I sowed cucumbers (those delightful lunch-box sized ones called *'Rocky',*) parsley, bergamot (Pimms anyone?) auricula primroses, and the 'shoo fly plant' (*Nicandra physalodes*). Elsewhere, the summer wildflower meadow had germinated nicely as had the cornfield. The potatoes were showing green and the radishes were up. The hawthorn looked healthy with its buds breaking into a vivid green, and the philadelphus exhibited strong growth (it had looked dead for a while). The cottage garden was also progressing nicely. So, everything in the garden was rosy, but why was that nagging feeling in the back of my mind telling me if anything can go wrong, it will go wrong?

❀ ❀ ❀

      Although it was early in the year, watering was necessary, and sometimes it's surprising what gets flushed out. As I was watering the bed by the summer house a rat raced out from underneath. Now, I knew we had rats but had no idea of their size.

This one was a huge brown monster. It must have been all of forty-five centimetres from the tip of its nose to the tip of its tail. A male I guess. With unbelievable speed it ran over my feet, jumped onto the vegetable garden wall, ran along it at break-neck speed, careered off at the far corner and disappeared under a hole at the corner of the terrace. All this time I tried to squirt it with the hose, but it eluded me.

Now don't get me wrong. I don't have a grudge against rats personally, they do an incredible tidy up job for us; it's what they carry that is worrying. Rats' urine can make a person quite ill, and of course, if your dogs or cats aren't inoculated it can give them parvovirus, which is a killer.

Then the pond pump then decided to pack up. That was the end of the mountain stream and waterfall. After yet another visit to St John's Garden Centre aquatic department and a new pump promptly bought, came the nightmare of unscrewing rusty jubilee clips. Once that was accomplished came the episode of trying to work out the right sized connector. In the end I abandoned the connectors and fitted the pump directly to the pipe. It worked just as well. The old management adage holds true. KISS. Keep It Simple Stupid!

❀❀❀

We never realised just how long today would be. Evelyn and I spent the morning titivating the place a bit. This involved more sweeping, tidying, and generally clearing up. Evelyn's got a thing about this, although I'm more inclined to keep things loose around the seams. I don't think Evelyn will ever really get the 'wildlife friendly' ethos, dear of her.

Finally, at three-thirty in the afternoon, a van pulled up with Carol Klein in tow. Of course, when I say in tow, I don't mean literally in tow as though her car had broken down, I mean she was following closely behind. When she clambered out of her car, she looked exactly as she does on the television. She wore a blue baggy jumper (with arms much too long,) faded blue denim jeans with turn-ups, and stout working boots. On her head she sported an interesting dyed blonde spiky hair-do, gold loopy earrings, and a beaming smile that reminded me of the Cheshire Cat from Alice in Wonderland, or was it Through the Looking Glass? Carol is a real WYSIWYG, What You See Is What You Get. She is down to earth with a great sense of humour, and full of enthusiasm and energy. She's lovely.

After what seemed an eternity all the filming and sound equipment was bundled off the van and the fun could commence. It began with interviews, with Carol asking me roughly the same questions as Jo Hynes. But, there were three areas on which the production team wished to focus.

Firstly, they asked me about the book I was thinking of writing (the book that you are now holding, too many years after its conception.) Secondly, they focused on the cornfield for discussion with Carol. And finally, the hen's blue mushroom boxes of turf.

George, the director wanted to begin the filming in the vegetable garden. Carol and I stood in front of the hen house while the cameraman, soundman, and George positioned themselves on the outside of the vegetable garden wall. On the word 'action,' our conversation began. It went something like this. Carol's opening gambit went as follows.

'Are you disappointed that you haven't got a place?'

'Yes, but really, when you look around, it's to be expected. There's so much space that needs filling.'

I must admit though that, in truth, I wasn't all that disappointed because all this had been discussed previously with Jo, and I never expected to be accepted anyway. This garden was still a work in progress.

With that, attention turned to the hen's turf boxes. With her wiggling index finger poking out of her over-long sleeve, she pointed to them and asked. 'Tell me about these strange blue boxes full of turf.'

'They're for the hens, Carol,' I replied. 'As you know, hens love scratching about on grass. So, because they do destroy the grass, we've worked out a rotation. We put in one box, and then when it's worn down we take it out and put in a fresh one.'

Moving on from that, Carol enthusiastically waved her arms about as she does and said, 'I think the great thing about this turf, is that when you've done with it, or rather when the hens have finished with it, you can stack it. It makes really good topsoil.'

I had no idea where I'd build these ever growing topsoil stacks, but I didn't say anything.

Glancing at the cornfield, Carol's face unexpectedly lit up as she had a bright idea. She said. 'Couldn't you use it along this narrow border you've got here? You could plant a native hedge. It would be like a field margin with this cornfield in front of it.'

'That's a good idea.' I replied.

'I think it would work brilliantly well.'

No sooner had she said this then Carol's ever active mind went onto something else.

She continued, hardly drawing breath. 'You know, there are so many places in your garden you could exploit too.'

'Oh yes,' I mumbled, trying to keep up with Carol's express train mind.

'I reckon if you upturned turf onto this,' she waived her hand in the general direction of the forward slanting pent roof of the small tool shed, 'you know, make it nice and deep, then just sow your seed, broadcast it right over the top. Get some sand too, couldn't you, to throw up there and grow thrift and sedums, all that kind of stuff. That'd be great wouldn't it?'

'Yea it would. That'd be great.'

Finally, the last filming of the evening comprised Carol's parting comments.

'I just think your garden is so inspiring. I really hope that when the county organiser returns, she's going to be so impressed, she'll be rushing to open the garden.'

After that gushing enthusiasm, all I could respond with was a wimpish, 'Thank you Carol.'

Besides all the thrill and discipline of the filming, lots of other things went on during this time. Early on, one of my friends turned up with his camera, wandered into the garden, and began his own filming. Dave behaved as though he was a man from the press, a member of the East The Water paparazzi. He photographed me, the film crew, and Carol with no sign of embarrassment at all.

Meanwhile, Carol and I became highly excited when a charm of goldfinches flew through the garden. She then had the film crew running around when a holly blue butterfly arrived. They tried their hardest to capture it on film but it was too fast for them. Evelyn found a brown caterpillar that Carol thought maybe a small tortoiseshell. That was filmed in close-up. Later an orange tip butterfly fluttered in and promptly fluttered out again. Greenfinches engaged in heated exchanges in the old elder.

On one occasion, I found a young greenfinch dead on the greenhouse staging among the cucumbers, peppers and begonias. It was perfect in form, not a feather out of place. I was surprised by the length of its claws. It must have flown into the greenhouse after being startled at the feeder and broke its neck colliding with the glass. It was so beautiful and delicate, and such a waste of a young avian life.

Plenty of insects inhabited the birch tree; in fact the birch is host to over 330 associated insect species. The quarrel of sparrows was nesting in the nest boxes. And hoverflies were in abundance. The garden was certainly crowded that evening. At 8.00 pm, filming day two was over and the overall feeling was one of exhaustion. So, after everyone was gone it was time to sit back on the terrace and enjoy a large vodka and orange, after all, all was well with the world. Well, my part of the world anyway, I couldn't say what it was like in anyone else's.

❀❀❀

The following day, by way of relaxation after that hard days filming, I cruised over to Barnstaple and checked out the garden centres in the locality, just to see what was about you'll understand.

Unfortunately, it should be made illegal for me to go anywhere near these places unaccompanied. At St John's Garden Centre I came away with, wait for it; a Rudbeckia deamii, a dwarf phlox, a border fork and spade (beautiful wooden handles and shafts, plus stainless steel tines and blade, they looked really Victorian,) a Felco leather secateurs holster (so that I can look the part on television, even if I didn't have any Felco secateurs,) two metal pyramid plant supports, a small cast iron birdbath, and a bundle of ten, two metre bamboo canes. A visit to B. J's Value House saw me walk away with a pot of ten Prunus Cerasifera (cherry plum or Myrobalan) for a hedge along the driveway. My wallet was somewhat lighter on the way home than when I left a few hours earlier. Possibly, the equation may be worked out that the reduced weight of my wallet equals increased petrol saving in my car, but it probably doesn't.

My shrub buying mania hadn't finished there. I next went online and bought four hawthorns for £12.50 plus postage and packing. That equates to about £3.12 each, more or less. Utter madness, but then I did have the bit between my teeth and was at full charge.

At this point, because we were continually working towards filming day deadlines, the garden began to feel more like a chore than a pleasure. No sooner had we relaxed then it was time to get back to the grindstone. A letter from the production company requested a garden plan. This took time as I walked round the garden trying to make sure I had the dimensions right and that everything was in the correct place. I used my garden design drawing skills to put the plan to paper. I duly sent it off for them to put in the programme when describing the garden.

The pressure was now on. On just one day, the 25th, petunias were pinched out, antirrhinums arranged in the cold frame, runner beans sowed in toilet rolls, an heirloom variety of tall pea named "purple podded," was sown into a length of guttering, nasturtiums, and courgettes into individual pots. Tagetes were potted on, the Prunus whips were potted up, and the cucumbers went into the greenhouse. Six broad beans were planted out in their toilet roll tubes and six more were sown in situ to see which would be the more successful. The pots of agapanthus were brought up from outside the writing shed and stationed in front of the wall by the arch on the terrace.

Turning attention to the trough in the prospective courtyard, things needed to be prepared for the next filming day. I knew that one of the sessions was going to centre on the planting of the trough, therefore I filled it out with the brunnaria, the primroses, Japanese anemones, ferns, scabious, and skyrocket conifer. They were kept in their pots so that they could be removed again for filming.

My non-existent DIY skills were now needed. I assembled together various lengths of 5x2.5 centimetre batten and constructed a frame to carry the bamboo screen that would go against the fence in the beach area. Fortunately, the quality of construction wasn't important because it would be screened by the screen. Thank goodness for that wonderful invention, the staple gun. Just hold it to the surface and squeeze the trigger. Bang, bang, bang, in go the staples. The job was done, but with a painful hand and wrist cramp.

I grouped pots of lilies together outside the writing shed door. Normally, I wouldn't give lilies house space because I don't like them. Their pollen is poisonous to cats and ruins ones' clothes with a shocking orange/yellow pollen stain that is impossible to remove.

These had been sent up from whom we call "them down below," to pinch a phrase from Laurie Lee's "Cider with Rosie." Them down below comprised of, my old mother, my older brother, who lived with her, and my older sister. They all lived in a sheltered housing estate at the bottom of the hill, and on a regular basis would send up all manner of goodies, from books, magazines, food, and you've guessed it, seeds and plants. But that's my family. They buy seeds and plants for us without asking us what we want or even don't want. Even when the garden is jammed full, plants still arrive. Sometimes they are in reasonable shape, sometimes they need intensive care, and sometimes they are dead and head for the mortuary at the bottom of the garden – the compost bin. It's like most things; generosity is a wonderful quality except when uncontrolled.

❀❀❀

The month was coming to an end so I thought a day of relaxation was in order. The Royal Horticultural Society (RHS) was holding a wildlife day on the Saturday so I went along with my friend Bill. He was getting on a bit, 85 years old at the time but still game for anything. He was a Lancaster pilot during the Second World War, was shot down, and spent some time in a Prisoner of War camp in Poland. But that's a different story. I'll be writing about that in the future.

The first lecture of the day was given by Chris Bailes, the curator of RHS Rosemoor. I was taken totally by surprise when he started promoting the case of small town gardens becoming an ideal environment for wildlife havens. It was exactly what I aimed to promote with my garden. During the lecture he expounded the ten top tips for helping us go wild in the garden. They are, to quote the handout:

1) Nurture a range of garden habitats (grass, pond, hedge, trees, etc.,) however small individually. A diverse garden is healthier, as is the right plant in the right place, reducing the need for pesticides and fertilisers.
2) Provide homes for wildlife. Bird and bat boxes are familiar, but how about a sculptural log-pile for the mini-beasts (the predators that will eat your pests!) And remember to put a bell on the cat. You don't want your birds eaten too.
3) Turn part of your lawn into a mini-meadow to encourage wild flowers and animals. You may get some lovely surprises, like a rare orchid or butterfly. Remember that birds love moss for nesting (think natural pampers.)

4) Grow plants for nectar, pollen, fruit, and seed, throughout the year. They'll attract more wildlife than bird feeders alone. And how about your own food needs? Home-grown food is more nutritious, as well as good green fun.

5) Create a water feature, however small. Whether pond or birdbath, all sorts of wildlife will be drawn to the oasis. Save the air miles and go "little game hunting" down at your very own watering hole. Don't forget your camera!

6) Save the burden on our sewers, as well as your wallet, and harvest the rain. Whether from your pond, tank or water butt, your plants will prefer natural water. They'll also like it if you mulch around them, holding that water.

7) Conserve vital nutrients too: home compost kitchen scraps and garden waste. It's better than the council having to do it and it's free. Compost heaps are also whole food chains in themselves.

8) Think about emissions (your carbon footprint, not your compost.) Choose garden products for energy efficiency – both in manufacture and use. Impress with funky recycled or reclaimed creations. They're the new black!

9) Ensure nothing you buy is putting a habitat under threat elsewhere in the world. Look for eco-certification. It's silly to exploit resources like peat or tropical hardwoods when there are more sustainable alternatives.

10) Develop a safe haven in which to relax, open your eyes and heart, and breathe deeply. Enjoy the wild beauty that's always there for you. Take the 'fence' away. Reconnect with your environment. Become whole.

I'll give him his due, Chris Bailes was a good lecturer. He used choice words, descriptive words; good Anglo-Saxon words for the most part.

During a break between lectures we strolled among the stalls. All kinds of organisations were there and many wares were on offer.

The Devon Wildlife Trust was prominent and so we headed for that. Much to my surprise Tom Hynes, the husband of Jo Hynes, the county assistant organiser, was there. He was friendly and we had a chat, during which he invited us to visit their garden on their next open day. We promised to. I had it in my mind to see their garden anyway, just to see how the higher echelons of the NGS perform. They judge us, but it might be interesting to put the boot on the other foot and judge them. Not harshly of course, but just to see what it's like.

During this stroll around I discovered a stall run by the British Lichen Society. Now this is a form of plant life I had hardly given a thought to – lichens. We see them all the time but never notice them. They are literally everywhere and I learned a lot in my chat with them.

For example, the ones we are most likely to be familiar with are the *crustose* type. These are the flat yellow, brown, and grey/green ones that look like tiny cow-pats and grow on bricks and mortar, gravestones, and concrete (there's that word again.) Then there are the *fruiticose* type, the fluffy ones that grow and hang around on old wooden benches, tree trunks, and twigs. They can tell us what our environment is like too. If you have the shrubby Beard lichen (*Usnea*), that's the blue dangly one that hangs off trees and shrubs, then it's a sure sign you're breathing clean air. Contrary to that, if you have an abundance of the orange leafy type of lichen, *Xanthoria parietina*, that's a sign of a nitrogen rich atmosphere from dust and car exhausts.

Lichens look like they should be horrible things to have on your stone, woodwork and trees, but nothing could be farther from the truth. They harm nothing; they are not parasites, but symbiotic organisms. Lichens are minute photosynthesising algal cells that live in harmony with microscopic fungi whose fungal threads take up moisture and give the body its shape. In that way both benefit from the relationship. And they are valuable in a multitude of ways. They are used by birds to build nests, used by the pharmaceutical industry to make antibiotics, and for making dyes. And to top it all, they made a garden look mature and lived in, adding atmosphere and extra interest.

All too soon it was time to set off back to the hall for the main lecture. Much to my surprise the lecturer was Dr Gavin Haig, the man who had influenced me the previous year on my visit to his garden when open for the NGS.

Bill and I approached him before the lecture and made ourselves known to him. He remembered me by the nickname he had given me when chatting to him previously. I am Sir Henry! We then settled down for the meat of the meeting. His lecture was full of humour, but not to the expense of depth. He stressed that nature is a gift to us and we should do all in our power to work with it, not abuse and ruin it. The thrust running all the way through was the balance of nature. We destroy it at our peril. That's a mantra which would be good for governments and big business to keep in mind.

Shortly before the end there was a sound like someone running their fingernails across the surface of a balloon. Immediately a familiar warm smell permeated the room. Bill had farted! All eyes turned towards him and his cheeks went as pink as Barbie's bathing suit.

So that was the end of April, a hectic and full month. I felt invigorated by going to the RHS wildlife day, but now it was time to for Evelyn and I to get our heads together for next month's filming deadline. May was going to be busy.

CHAPTER SIX

MAY

According to an old epithet, the two iffy months previous to May are somehow supposed to be beneficial. "March winds and April showers bring forth May flowers," so we're told. We were full of anticipation, particularly as another proverb says, "Dry May, wet June" And indeed, May had come in dry, and we had flowers, but maybe it was just a tad too hot, especially for those young plants in the green house.

The poor little seedlings and plants were under pressure. We had to start an intensive, twice a day, watering regime; first thing in the morning and last thing at night. Watering during the heat of the day would have been lethal. Water on the plants under the intense rays of the sun would have scorched the leaves to a crisp, and boiled the roots of the poor things to cooked vegetables.

After a good rummage around in the potting shed, the shed where during the course of the winter everything gets cast, I managed to find the white chalklike shading known as Coolglass that I paint on the greenhouse panes every year. Every year I kept meaning to get a permanent shading system of blinds, but I never get round to it. This whitewash stuff is fine, but on the side of the greenhouse everyone rubs against it and it comes off on their clothes. Fortunately, it doesn't stain or damage, but it means I've got to paint the damn side panes again… and again… and again. Still, it had to be done. We couldn't afford to lose what would help to sell the garden to Jo Hynes when she made her final visit.

❀ ❀ ❀

This premature heat had drawn out a number of early flyers. Holly blue butterflies continued to come through the garden investigating our holly and ivy. An orange tip butterfly occasionally fluttered and dipped its zig-zag way across the cottage garden bed looking for a female (only the male has the distinctive orange tip to their wings.) When mated, the females look for plants of the cabbage family on which to lay their eggs. Not the usual brassicas fortunately but the spring flowers of the large bittercress, garlic mustard, and cuckoo flower. It's such a shame that such beauty is so short-lived, the adults (or imagos as the adults are technically known) only live 18 days at most. We even had a Red Admiral bless us with a visit. Arriving from the continent in May means that these migrants will have an early start in producing a resident population in the summer.

The cotoneaster by the driveway wall was being relished by all sorts of insects and bees. The honey bee, the buff-tailed bumblebee (*Bombus terrestris,*) the white-tailed bumblebee (*Bombus lucorum,*) the red mason bee (*Osmia rufa,*) and numerous hoverflies were gorging themselves on the copious nectar being produced, and the plentiful pollen being collected by the bees would satisfy even the hungriest bee grubs. I also spotted a hornet on there. My field guide said that it's Britain's largest wasp at 1 ¼ inches, but is under pressure and becoming rarer. Unfortunately, everything is becoming rarer. It's so disappointing that man is degrading his environment so rapidly. Dr Haig's lecture came to mind again.

To follow the cotoneaster is a white single-flowered member of the Tea Tree family (*Leptospermum polygalifolium.*) Again, the bees and hoverflies savour the tiny cup-like flowers for weeks.

It was exciting to know that the organic, wildlife friendly regime was working because I recognised plenty of the hoverfly, *Syrphus Ribesii*, in the air, and even on the lily pads in the pond. This is a welcome hoverfly because it eats 800 aphids during its two-week larval stage.

I noticed too that the fascinating little character of the Lepidoptera world, Willoughby's leafcutter bee (*Megachile willughbiella*) was out and about. She had been taking sections of the everlasting pea, but as yet had not touched the roses. It's an intriguing sight to watch her cut perfectly semi-circular sections from the edge of a leaf, roll it into a tube, and then fly off like a bomber with a torpedo along the length of her undercarriage. Carrying this weight made her rather heavy so she flew quite slowly and had to stop at intervals to catch her breath. This gave me the opportunity to follow her. To my surprise she made for the greenhouse. When inside the greenhouse she targeted an old fifteen centimetre clay pot, un-emptied from last year. The compost contents had dried out and shrunk away from the sides leaving easy access for her to dig down the sides and create a space for the tubes of leaf. Into this she would lay the solitary egg to become the next generation. When accomplished, sadly, she would fly away and then die. Needless to say, that pot stayed there all summer untouched by human hand, or any other hand come to think of it, until the following spring when we emptied it and were amazed with what we saw. Numerous perfect little leaf-tubes were set into the hard-baked potting compost. It's one of those occasions that make one in awe of wildlife and its instinctive intelligence.

During May, the birds were a fine example of industry. One day, while walking around the garden, the liners of the hanging baskets appeared somewhat ragged and tatty, as though they had put their fingers into an electric socket (if they had fingers of course, which they haven't.) It was as though someone had been plucking them. And they had. After lying in wait for a while, we discovered the culprits. The sparrows were pulling out the fibres for nesting material. It's interesting that the sparrow is the same family as the weaver birds of Africa. But, whereas the weaver birds make carefully woven and intricate nests, if you look at a sparrow's, it's just the opposite. It looks thrown together and stamped about on for a bit. One nest made by a craftsman and the other by a labourer.

The parenting instinct is strong, and fledglings were hidden all over the garden. The blackbird youngster was hiding in a patch of ivy with merely its gentle contact call of "pip-pip-pip" giving away its location. Greenfinches were well on in the feeding education process with both adult and juveniles busily scoffing at the feeders. Sparrow fledglings are a demanding bunch. There were a number of families around the feeders with mum and dad pursuing a hectic round of feeding the youngsters who constantly flapped their wings in their "feed me" fashion. A fledgling dunnock was in the vegetable garden jumping from pot to pot. It was quite young because of the tufty hair pieces on the side of its head. It kept trying to fly, but badly. Again and again it crashed into the henhouse, but appeared none the worse for it.

Life is so full of jeopardy for the youngsters and mortality is high. Of most birds that frequent our gardens, only about 10% - 20% will survive long enough to breed the following year. The adults don't fare much better. It's estimated that the passerine life span is about 1 ¼ to 1 ½ years. So that robin you see each year and think is the same one, in all probability isn't. Although for three years we did have a one footed female blackbird with us, which was great fun.

Strangely, there is an emotional side to wildlife gardening. It brings a sense of wellbeing and you become attached to "your" sparrows, "your" song thrush, and "your" robin. You get involved with their lives. Okay, they are "yours" in a way, but as far as they are concerned, they see the bigger picture. Our gardens are just a part of their territory, but if we can make our gardens the central part of their territory, that truly is satisfying. There is a magic in the music of the bees, insects, and birds that fill a wildlife garden. The song of the blackbird, the trill of the robin, the inharmonious cackling of the house sparrow choir, the buzzing of the insects; all is totally discordant, but somehow pleasing and satisfying to listen too. In fact, it could be said that nature is a work of art. All the flora and fauna fit together with different shapes, textures, and colours making each garden a unique jigsaw masterpiece; no two gardens are ever the same, nature is fond of variety. Nature is fascinating as everywhere you look you can see living creatures getting on with their busy lives. There is a tremendous sense of wonder and awe when we discover something new. When I first came across the caterpillar of the Vapourer moth, I was stunned. Look it up in a field guide and you'll see why. There's always something different happening too. One afternoon a sparrow hawk gave the garden a visit and was promptly mobbed by jackdaws. And I've never seen sparrows move so fast either. One second they were at their noisy best and all over the place. The next second there was neither sight nor sound of them. The quarrel had gone to ground. There's excitement in watching the next generation of sparrows or blackbirds or blue tits being raised in your garden. You actually feel part of the "whole," a part of the real world, and not a stranger cut off and living in an artificial and lonely bubble.

❀ ❀ ❀

The garden was now coming into its own. With its strong musky scent, the Californian lilac (*Ceanothus dentatus*) was in flower and attracting the bees, as was what I call the English lilac (*Syringa x chinensis*,) or the Rouen lilac, again with its own unmistakable perfume; a perfume that epitomises an English spring.

The cottage garden bed was edged with granny bonnets (*Aquilegia* cultivars) and they were in full flower, including "Black Barlow" and "Nora Barlow". Apparently, Nora Barlow was Charles Darwin's niece.

The greenhouse was packed with exuberant seedlings and burgeoning plants. If glass were elastic, it would be stretched to bursting point. The time had come for action. It was time to do the hanging baskets and troughs. Even if it was technically too early, I had to plant them up and clear the space.

Out came the lobelias, petunias, pelargoniums and nasturtiums. This year to add to the pressure, I had promised my friend Bill, that I would do his three hanging baskets for him. This duty duly executed, I ventured onto my own.

For the first time ever, I was making a basket out of moss with plants sticking out from the sides. It looked a bit odd, but hopefully the plants will grow and thicken to make it look more of a sphere eventually. Other than that, I finally ended with nine hanging baskets, eight large troughs, and ten bulky terra-cotta and clay pots, all primed with promise of summer.

So finally the greenhouse was empty... ish. The staging was cleared and the border dug over and levelled. Into six eight-inch pots went two bell peppers, two aubergines, and two cucumbers. Into six twelve-inch pots went our heritage tomatoes, "Harbinger."

One Sunday afternoon we thought we would have lunch out at a garden centre. We choose "Merry Harriers" near the village of Woolfardisworthy, (the name of which is reduced to Woolsery by the locals for obvious reasons.) You know exactly what I'm going to say next don't you? Yes, I've said it before, and I'm about to say it again, I should never be set free in a garden centre without some kind of supervision.

Sitting proudly in the back of the car on the way home were a woodland cranesbill (*Geranium sylvaticum*,) a variegated oregano (the bees love it,) a sage (because the frost killed the last one,) and a weigelia (no idea where to plant it, but the bees love it.) Still, hey ho.

❀❀❀

One morning, I sat in my writing shed hunched over the desk while contemplating what to do with the outline of a short story, when, from my periphery vision, I became conscious of something moving up the elder tree just outside the window. Glancing up I watched a huge fat brown rat climb up the trunk and launch itself into the tray of the bird feeder. It swung backwards and forwards as though on a boat-swing at the fairground. After the swinging had settled, I stared at it, and it stared back at me, totally unconcerned, just stuffing its huge ratty face with my bird's seed. I went out to have words with him but he just jumped back onto the elder in a cloud of birdseed, scurried down the trunk, and away under the writing shed.

A few days later, his demise happened quite out of the blue. Our friend Lee had come for lunch, and afterwards we went for a walk around the garden to show her how things were progressing.

We had reached the wildflower meadow and were discussing what it contained when the dogs kicked off big time. They had been showing interest at the Belfast sink beside the greenhouse with plenty of sniffling and snuffling, but now it was full on barking and yapping. Unexpectedly, from under the sink, the big brown rat made a run for it, straight up the centre path, heading for a clump of bulky ferns. They both made a dash at it and disappeared into the ferns amid barking and ratty type squeals. Bonnie had the edge and came out with the rat in her jaws while Toto ran about in approbation. She gave it a good shaking and trotted round the top of the garden and then came back down the fruit tree avenue towards the greenhouse. There, on my command, she dropped it. It lay on its back with its little feet sticking up in the air. I was horrified to discover that it was still breathing. It filled me with dread. That meant I would have to dispatch it myself; I had told Bonnie to leave it too early.

Now, I'm not very good at killing things. I can't even kill my hens after they've come to the end of their productive life. They just become pets until they die of old age. But, here I was surrounded by two excited dogs and two human spectators intrigued with what I was going to do next. I went to get a spade to "dap 'en on the 'ead," a phrase Devonians use as a euphemism for killing something.

I was saved the torment of putting it out of its misery though. It must have attended the rodent equivalent of the Royal Academy of Dramatic Arts, because as I approached it, ratty gave one of those huge theatrical dying breaths, and expired. He deserved a posthumous Oscar for that performance.

A few days later we caught a small rat in the trap set by the terrace flowerbed, they had been tunnelling under the steps. Bonnie got there first and ate most of it leaving sticky, blood-stained whiskers on her face. Another rat had been tormenting her for ages at the same place. She could regularly see its little black beady eyes peering up at her through the gaps in the slabs. As in all life though, it only takes one mistake. And that one mistake for this particular rat was to be discovered out in the open by the pond one afternoon. Bonnie chased it into the pond and after much splashing and upheaval the little terrier surfaced with one dead soaking wet rat.

The compost heap and leaf mould bins were very popular with rat families as a perfect place to call home. But life can be treacherous there too. We once found a number of baby rats dead, drowned in a watering can in the greenhouse.

It's a shame to kill them; after all, they were created to be nature's dustbin men. And, like with most creatures, they can only populate to the sustainable level of food supplies. They're as much a part of the food web as anything else. But, what with neighbours, and the risk of rat borne disease, sadly, there's no room for live and let live.

⊛⊛⊛

I have a German friend named Falk Hanisch. During the time of that country's division, he lived in East Germany, did his time of national service in the armoured corps as a tank driver, and learned to be a plumber by trade. When the Berlin wall came down and the country was unified, he became a European citizen and could then move freely within the European Union, which he did. It was while he lived and worked in Majorca that he met and married an English woman, Lisa, and had a child, Anna. Naturally they gravitated to England and settled here in North Devon, where most of her family lived.

As it turned out they came to the same congregation of Jehovah's Witnesses as Evelyn and me and we became friends. I knew things were hard for them in the economic situation of the time; he only had low paid part-time work, so I put a suggestion to him. Perhaps he would like to build the wall of the enclosure we were planning? He agreed to, and the deal was complete. It was time for the courtyard, part two; its completion.

Before he could start though, we had to bring in the needed materials. Therefore, my hard working car and trailer were put to use as a donkey and cart. I went to the local builder's merchants and collected forty concrete blocks. These were collected in two runs of twenty because I only have a small trailer and the poor little tyres looked as though they were running flat under the weight, ready to burst any minute. The third visit involved picking up twenty-five bags of sand, and five bags of cement. That gave a ratio of a 5:1 mix for the mortar. My fourth and final journey was to the hire department of the builder's merchants, where I signed up for a cement mixer and duly brought it back.

Falk made a good start. He began the three metre run along the boundary between our next-door neighbours and our driveway. There, he turned at a right angle and made his way across the driveway. At this point Evelyn decided that if we installed a two metre gate it would be a proper courtyard rather than just an enclosure. That gave me the inspiration to use it as an example of what can be done in a town courtyard garden to help wildlife. No garden is too small to help wildlife and nearly all new gardens in the new estates are small courtyards.

In many ways, we've got ourselves into this parlous state regarding the natural world because of the misinterpretation of a single verse in the Bible, Genesis 1:28, where it says we should subdue the earth and have all living creatures in subjection. Unfortunately, as usual, imperfect man has overstepped the mark and taken this to the extreme. Subdue can mean two things, either to moderate, in other words keep under control, soften, quieten down, or conversely, to beat down, crush, trample. Yes, left to itself, the earth would be overgrown and ungoverned, but it can be subdued gently as in the first instance by working with nature, it can be handled sensitively and benevolently. But instead, we treat the earth as in the latter instance. We treat it as though we were tyrants; we bully it, and ride rough shod over it.

So yes, we are the most predominant of creation because we are the most intelligent and powerful. But that gives us the responsibility to care for the natural world and not exploit it to extinction. When we are doing things to our environment we should be sympathetic to the wildlife and work around it and with it, not just crush it out of existence. When we build housing estates, or even new towns (which aren't necessarily bad projects in themselves) they should be wildlife friendly with gardens and green spaces for all to enjoy. Grey concrete diminishes a person's life but green space enhances it. Why oh why can't architects design buildings with green roofs and hanging gardens? Architects seem to lack real imagination. Essentially it's all about empathy; we need to look at the world from wildlife's perspective. We need to abandon our selfishness and understand nature and its wants and needs, then work with it. Slowly, oh so slowly, some people are beginning to recognise this more and more. And that was the philosophy behind the courtyard garden. I would use it to teach visitors what can be done to help wildlife in the small town gardens that exist today.

Thankfully, Falk didn't complete it in one day; and he wouldn't be back for a while. He wanted to let the first layers of blocks set hard before going higher, and besides, he had to catch up on his other work. That was a blessing really, because the gates were going to be a peculiar size. My research on the Internet revealed that double gates are usually two metres, forty-five centimetres, and single gates are one metre, twenty centimetres. Still, Evelyn was adamant that the gate should be two metres exactly, even if it was a bastard size.

That led us onto a wild-goose chase in search of gates. We went to the re-cycling centre at Caddesdown in Bideford... nothing. We went to the re-cycling centre at Deep Moor in Torrington... nothing. We called in at Iron Craft on the way to Barnstaple... nothing, they were just closing. We drove on to Guy Windsor Metal works... nothing; they were closed and according to a neighbour, away for the weekend. Finally, we set anchor at B&Qs in Barnstaple, where we paid a ridiculous price for two single gates with the hare-brained idea of making them into a double gate. At least we now had a pair of gates and an idea of what we wanted to do with them.

On the way home we dropped by on Gerald and Marian Ley, Evelyn's sister and her husband. Gerald was something of a self-taught engineer and could put his hand to anything constructive. His workshop was enthralling; it was an Aladdin's cave of tools and equipment. We asked him if he could help and he immediately said yes. In his mind's eye he could see exactly what we wanted and grasped the idea quite readily. He even offered some suggestions.

❀ ❀ ❀

The third filming day was imminent. It was time for a clear up. Unfortunately, the day turned out to be lousy. It was a litany of disaster. I let the morning drift until 9.45 so I got miserable. And because I got miserable, things began to go wrong. The potting compost I was removing from the courtyard to the potting shed fell off the trolley with great regularity. The trolley went through unnoticed dog-poo. Unnoticed that is, until it stuck to the trolley wheels and was spread around, this, in the process, created a great stink to rival anything from the medieval River Thames. Finally, one of the bags got pierced by a stick and left what looked like a trail of gunpowder that ran along the path.

I had a chance to note that the cherry-plum plants I had potted up to grow on in a beautiful terra-cotta pot were vigorously sending out new roots. I didn't have X-Ray vision, but was evidenced when Toto raced around, knocked it over, and smashed it in his excitement.

As the day continued my potting shed slowly filled. Plastic fencing, stray pots, wheelbarrows, bamboo canes, all things that distract from the visual image ended up in my poor old sanctum. Finally, just to finish off, I had to move the remains of the sand, cement, and concrete blocks to a discreet corner so that they wouldn't be caught in camera shot. We ended the day absolutely exhausted and not looking forward to tomorrow's filming.

❀ ❀ ❀

The day came in dismal, overcast, and threatening rain. The film crew arrived at 10.30 am prompt. There were only three of them, George (the assistant producer,) Stuart (the cameraman,) and Jimmy (the soundman.) By their air of industry, I could tell we were lined up for an intensive four-hour session.

It was to be a day of interviews and two action sequences. The first action sequence involved the dead-heading of the granny bonnets. The second was the planting up of the courtyard trough. This was to be followed by Evelyn's, and my, interviews.

It was during the dead-heading that I discovered the truth about the old adage which says you can't believe everything you see on television. We went to the fruit tree avenue with the edging of aquilegias, all standing in a line sporting a fine display of seed heads. The cameraman asked me to walk along doing the dead-heading while he filmed me at a low level, giving a film sequence level with the action. This duly done, I waited to go onto the next item.

Unexpectedly he grinned and piped up with, 'Sorry could we do that again? I'm not very happy with what I got there.'

I stared at him with furrowed eyebrows. 'How can we do it again? I've cut them all off. There aren't any more to do.'

'Don't you worry about that,' he countered, 'just poke the stems back into the clump of leaves and pretend to dead-head them.'

I did as I was told and on the word 'action' I wandered along the row thrusting my secateurs into the plants cutting imaginary stems invisible to the camera, and then pulling out the result, an already cut stem. And I did this all along the row, although on film it looked as if it was happening then and there.

The second action sequence took place in the courtyard. In this instance they wanted me to plant up the trough. Therefore, I took the plants out that I had placed in there previously and then replanted them while being interviewed. I came out with the ridiculous comment, while trying to be funny, that if Jo Hynes didn't accept me his time, I would put her under a harsh light and put matchsticks under her fingernails. As soon as I said it I realised that it wasn't funny and could be taken the wrong way. And knowing it was now on film, I had to plead with them not to use that part but to cut it and dump it, which they kindly agreed to do.

I'm a real gobbo sometimes. My mouth works faster than my brain. That wasn't the first time in my life that I've come out with something and wished I hadn't. While trying to be quick-witted and amusing, I can occasionally come out with something that's dim-witted and unamusing. Still, that's me I guess. Anyway, it didn't matter in the end; the final programme didn't have that interview and action sequence in it, thank goodness.

Evelyn's interview came next on the agenda. She sat on a seat on the lawn and answered the producer's questions. I think the final programme only used about two sentences from about quarter of an hour's filming. I've always thought that there's an awful lot of waste when making television programmes, both in film and time. This experience proved it. Hours can be spent with the result of just a couple of minutes, or less, of used film.

The weather blessed us while we were filming the action and outdoor interviews. And, although overcast and dire for the most part, the rain held off and gifted us occasional glimpses of the sun.

My final interview was to be held in the doghouse. I sat in the doorway while the crew squatted down on the path outside. Unfortunately for the crew though, the weather finally closed in and the skies opened. While I sat cosily in the dry, the three of them became soaked through. Still, I'll give them their due. They weren't namby-pamby types; they sat it out, gritted their teeth, kept calm, and carried on, still with a sense of humour. Again we took quite a while for less than a minute's usable product; all that was included in the final production was a short comment where I said that everybody thinks you need four or five acres to do things for wildlife, but you don't. You can do things for wildlife in a town garden just by the plants you use and the way you arrange it. And a final sentence where I said that if we got into the Yellow Book it would be a real sense of accomplishment.

I must mention some of the equipment they used. Firstly, the sound equipment had such a fine sensitivity that it was affected by the birdsong emanating from a quarrel of sparrows that inhabit our garden and fly around chattering to each other in their gregarious way. Noises from the town traffic affected it likewise. Every time a vehicle went past we had to stop, and then start again. On one occasion, one of my neighbours from across the road and a few houses down was cutting his grass, but even that disturbed the sound. One of the crew was dispatched to tell him that we were filming and could he put off cutting his grass until later. A bit cheeky, but he did it!

The long, flowing shots were done by using an Australian invention called a "Trolley Dolly." It consisted of a short set of flexible tubular light-weight railway tracks on which sat a tripod with three castors in one unit on each leg to carry the camera.

Rising and falling aerial shots were filmed by fixing the camera onto a crane like contraption called a mini-jib. This rose and fell smoothly by means of a weighted counter balance at the rear. Filmed with a wide-angle lens the scene appears higher than it, in truth, is.

All these bits of kit take some skill to use. I was most impressed. And using this equipment they spent the rest of the visit filming the progress of the garden to show how it is growing.

Finally, at just after mid-afternoon, we bid George, Stuart, and Jimmy a fine farewell until next time and they set off for Swansea in Wales to stay over and start the next day's filming first thing in the morning.

❀❀❀

At last we had our garden to ourselves. Or so we thought. Just after filming Gerald Ley turned up to inspect the site of the courtyard gates and we ended up giving him a guided tour of the garden. Then, just as he was leaving, our neighbour Graham arrived, and we gave him a tour as well.

There was no filming planned for the next month, but that didn't mean it was going to be a quiet one.

CHAPTER SEVEN

JUNE

Hurrah Hussar, no filming this month! Four weeks respite. Therefore, we thought that we'd enjoy a bit of down time and relax by visiting a couple of local National Garden Scheme gardens. We could even get a few ideas we might steal for our garden.

The first place we headed for was Jo Hynes' garden at Higher Cherubeer, near Dolton. It was part of a joint opening, which included two other gardens in the rural community, Cherubeer itself, and Middle Cherubeer. They were all part of Jo and Tom's family, they owned the hamlet.

After we had parked in the field at Higher Cherubeer, we met Jo at the gate where she was taking the money. Later, during our stroll round the garden, we met her husband Tom. He's something big in the North Devon Biosphere/Area of Outstanding Natural Beauty/Tarka trail sort of thing. Their garden was very well presented, but then you would expect nothing less from the assistant county organiser. The organiser's gardens must be the yardstick by which all the other gardens are measured.

The garden was about an acre, sitting as it did at 500 feet above sea level looking out across a south west facing valley. I was glad it wasn't mine; it would be hard to garden there, the site being so exposed and consisting of a stony, acid, clay soil.

The first area we discovered was Jo's wildlife garden. It was effectively a woodland glade with a winding walk through it. The path was made from roughly chipped bark and held together on each side by lengths of round rustic posts, eight centimetres in diameter, laid end to end, thereby creating a continuous edge to the walkway. Running along the side of the path were cranesbills in abundance and variety as an edging. We could see what an excellent woodland and border plant this was.

There was also small flowered Clematis, with a beautiful fragrance, climbing through the trees. I didn't know its cultivar, but it was of the group two type, because it was flowering in summer.

We noticed that the Hynes' kept the trunks of many trees and shrubs clear of lower branches. This raised the canopy slightly and let in the light, which encouraged the under-plantings to thrive. The result was that it gave a more realistic woodland edge effect.

About half way along the woodland walk, we came across the perfect woodpile. They had sawn logs into six-foot lengths or so, driven in four stakes to create a retaining structure, two on each side, leaving about four feet above ground. It was the shape of an ottoman, like an oblong box. The bit that was a stroke of genius was a hollow left about half way along that could be used as shelter or hibernacula for hedgehogs and other creatures. This was the credo of wildlife gardening; wood is good. Wood can be used all over the garden. It can be used for edging, log piles, compost bins, fencing, hedges, and chippings to makes paths or mulch, anywhere you can think of.

This garden holds the secret of year round interest. It has over 200 varieties of snowdrops, and the national collection of hardy cyclamen. That makes sure that even winter and early spring are full of interest.

The next garden belonged to Jo's mum, Janet Brown. This was the original Cherubeer, a beautiful little 15th century thatched cottage. The garden surrounded it on all sides. Arranged as small rooms there was something of interest in each. There were borders of perennials and herbs settled in among shrubs and trees. Again, there was a distinct woodland feel to it. Some of the rooms had a pond in them and another had a wonderful lump of architectural driftwood as its centrepiece. It was what I'd call a cosy garden.

The third garden of the trilogy, Middle Cherubeer, was Tom Hynes' mum and dad. Mum was called Heather, but I can't remember his dad's. This garden was smaller than the others, but was full of what I term wet interest. It was divided into three sections, one a mass of colourful perennials, one a bog garden, and the other a good effort at a wildlife pond. A goodly amount of paths connected them all together. A rather dilapidated summerhouse looked out across the valley and fields. Fabulous! Or rather, it would have been if it were in use. It was just full of old seating stuff, like a cupboard under the stairs or the general-purpose drawer, or my potting shed on filming days come to think of it.

It was a useful visit. We came away with ideas to raise the canopy of our shrubs to create a more realistic woodland edge, to make a well-structured log-pile, and to develop further the idea of garden rooms with interesting vistas and focal points.

Word gets around. When we were talking to Jo, she told us that the camera crew were quite excited about our garden and thought it a good one. That was encouraging.

❀ ❀ ❀

Two miles east of where we live, along one of the worse roads to travel in North Devon, is Webbery. The garden we were visiting was Little Webbery. At the time, it consisted of the big house and a small thatched cottage at the far end of the garden.

It was unusual in that it had a double ha!-ha!; it was quite an effective trick because one could look right down the garden to the countryside beyond giving the impression that it was all one piece of joined land. This is very effective in a country garden, but rubbish for a town one. Interestingly, the name Ha! Ha! comes from the French, and was first coined in 1712 by the French gardener, Alexander Le Blond who said in his book, The Theory and Practice of Gardening, that it was "an obstacle interrupting one's way sharply and disagreeably;" it… "Surprises… and makes one cry Ah! Ah!" The English, with their quirky sense of humour, anglicised the name and changed it from Ah! Ah! to Ha! Ha!

All in all, Little Webbery covered about three acres. The house sat in the southeast corner of the garden, which then stretched out to the north and west. It was as if a vast square had been plonked securely into the middle of the Devon countryside.

There was a huge lake and a smaller pond, but both were attractive and, overall, useful for wild life. A raised bank went along three sides of the pond with a path running between this bank and the edge of the pond. The lake was much further to the north-west.

Adjacent to the house was a series of garden rooms set out much like the flag of Sweden, an offset cross. It was in effect the old walled kitchen that had fallen from grace, as most of these large house kitchen gardens have done through the decades. Now it was set out as a rose garden with a series of beds surrounded by yew and box hedging.

All in all, it was a pleasant garden, but the gardening proper wasn't done by the proprietors. As is often the case with these larger houses and gardens, the actual gardening was done by the gardeners, or in this case, gardener; a lovely young person named Katrina. I asked her how she dealt with the garden, seeing as she was the lone gardener on three acres, and she said that she just starts at the top by the house and tried to work her way outwards. I could see the crafty logic in that. It always looks decent at the family's end, and it doesn't matter so much if the farthest parts aren't reached quite so often.

As we were due to leave, I drove the car from the car park to the gate to pick up Evelyn and Bill. On the way, I bumped into Jo Hynes, not literally of course, that could have turned a bit nasty. She was making her way towards the house. I wound down the window to speak to her.

'Hello,' I said. 'Fancy meeting you here.'

'Oh, hello,' she replied. 'I'm glad I've seen you. Miranda and I have been talking and there's a garden within about .9 of a kilometre of your house.'

'I see. Have you been on your GPS again?' That quip received no response.

'It's ideal because that means there's a possibility you could open as a pair. We like that sort of thing.'

Well, I didn't really like that sort of thing myself, but I kept my trap shut. Does that insinuate that our garden hasn't got forty-five minutes of interest? Blow me down, for those who are interested, it's got hours of interest.

When I got home I ran .9 of a kilometre through my computer converter and it came out as 0.559234073 miles, give or take an inch or so. But, when I drove it sometime later, my odometer in the car gave it more like well over a mile.

❀ ❀ ❀

At the beginning of the month, we felt it was time to complete the courtyard, but to start with, the trough had to be replanted properly. Therefore, the day after filming it all came up and went back in. This time with proper compost and feeding to give everything a good kick off.

Latterly, Falk arrived to finish off the courtyard wall. He was tired, and not in the best of health, owing to a painful shoulder that had been playing him up for weeks. This was revealed by the fact that the final part of the wall wasn't completed to the same standard as the rest. That's not meant to be a criticism, just an observation, because that would be the case with any of us doing a job and not feeling too good.

However, when he finished we had a chat over a cup of tea; a cup of tea that lasted in excess of forty-five minutes. It comprised, for virtually all that time, of the history of his relationship with his boss when he was doing his apprenticeship in East Germany. He finished off by explaining how this boss had treated him badly when making him redundant. Old wounds take a long time to heal, I suppose, but honestly, he could talk for England, or should that be Germany. It could probably be both actually. Falk is a lovely fellow and has become a great friend

The estimation of materials was a bit out. We still had four bags of cement and seven bags of sand left over, but that didn't matter. I hadn't finished our constructions yet.

Therefore, it was off to Jewson the builder's merchants for six concrete blocks and three bags of 20mm shingle. When I returned, I set to and built another raised bed, but this time in the corner of the courtyard instead of running it flush with the lower wall. The reason for this was that if the bed had been along the lower wall it would be at the bottom of the slope, become a rain trap, and then cause drainage problems. That was the purpose of the shingle, to create an attractive soak-away at the bottom of the slope.

I then had a pleasant trip to the garden centre and brought in two huge bales of potting compost, four bags of bark chippings (special offer,) a combination lock padlock, a one metre by two metre length of trellis, and a pack of variegated ivy. Stick with it, you never know what you'll come home with after a visit to a garden centre.

Anyhow, the afternoon saw me working like mad to get the courtyard complete. To begin with, I gave birth to the courtyard's new bed. I filled it with two bales of compost plus the two bags of St John's compost I had left over. That done, I fixed four, two-inch cubes of wood on the bottom wall, and then mounted the trellis on them. This kept the trellis proud of the wall for the *Clematis* "Sweet Sensation" to grow into and turn hopefully into a thick tangle that the birds will enjoy. How to keep the cats out will be another problem to address at some time in the future.

I then had a period of planting. The Lady of the Garden suggested that I use the *Polyanthus* and *Cineria* from the old hanging basket. That was a good idea for re-cycling plants. They had become exhausted in the basket, but in the ground, they could revitalise. I went on to plant the beautiful buttery yellow *Lysimachus* (bought during the visit to Webbery Gardens,) the ephemeral flowered *Cranesbill* "Blue cloud" (acquired at Cherubeer Gardens,) and a stately Bergamot (*Monarda*.) I can't remember where I got that from. Finally, I took a gamble and planted my last remaining hawthorn in the far corner of the corner bed. The remaining bag of compost was used to plant two huge, but elegant, terracotta pots. Into each pot went a *Cuppressus* "Goldcrest" and a couple of variegated ivies to dangle over the side in wonton abandon.

To finish off, I thought I would be clever and fix an eye plate on the corner of the long trough. This would be to chain my trailer, thereby avoiding its theft. The usual happened though. As I happily drilled away, the mortar shattered and fell like confetti around my feet. Too much sand and not enough cement again, dammit. I wasn't a happy bunny.

I then noticed that rain had washed some of the colouring off the wall. It must have rained pretty hard before it had dried. Dammit again.

✸✸✸

This month the garden lived up to its name. We were slowly seeing the fruits of our hard work as the blank beds began to turn into a garden. But the work continued, even though there was to be no filming this month.

Watering was a daily occurrence. Hanging baskets, pots, troughs, and the greenhouse all needed watering first thing in the morning. Moreover, if the day was particularly hot, then watering had to be done in the evening as well, especially the greenhouse.

We spent a good deal of time in the greenhouse getting it up to speed by making it presentable and clearing out the rubbish while tying in the tomatoes, peppers, and cucumbers, so that it at least looked a bit professional.

Rasputin, the Russian vine growing along the wire fence beside the driveway had to go. We called it that because it was almost impossible to kill. It can't be denied that it's pretty, but it lives up to its nick-name of the "mile a minute" plant. It even resembles the character of the country it's named after. It tries to take over everything it comes across in double quick time. It took nearly a week to accomplish and we regretted taking on the job a number times. It's one of those soul destroying jobs that go on, and on, and on, and on, and on; a bit like this sentence really.

The woodland edge effect in the shrubbery was created by doing what we had seen at Jo Hynes' garden. By lifting the canopy of the *vibernum bodnantense* "Dawn," and the *Genista* "Porlock" it let in more light and developed a more dappled effect.

The hanging baskets and borders were burgeoning with blooms. The petunia's trumpets blew their colourful tune, the trailing lobelia began to show their petals of delicate hew, and the deep flowered tubes of nicotiana shone in the dusky twilight attracting the long tongued moths. The tiny purple flowers of the toadflax and agastach attracted bees and butterflies galore, and the reds of the pink campion and foxglove were visited in rapid profusion by the bumblebees. The leptospermum that had taken over from the cotoneaster was crawling with innumerable varieties of bees and insects. I saw a beefly, an insect I had never seen before. It was brown with a fluffy elongated triangular shaped body. It had a prominent proboscis, easily the length of its body. It was like a needle on the front of its face. The whole thing was a joy to behold; the garden was a buzz with thousands of tiny wings.

Those with bigger wings were much in evidence too. The birds were intense in their activity. Our new prestigious visitors, the goldfinches, were using new niger feeder we had recently installed for them. Greenfinches were present as were blackbirds, dunnocks, house sparrows, blue tits, wrens, robins, starlings, chaffinches, collared doves and others who popped by for lunch. It was so satisfying. The sparrows, dunnocks and blackbirds in particular were being industrious. There was much coming and going at the sparrow terrace we had mounted under the eaves. The dunnock was nesting and bringing up fledglings in the conifer hedge, while the blackbird was doing the same in the escallonia hedge at the bottom of the garden. A sparrowhawk, with its grey back, orange barred chest, and piercing yellow eyes, came into the garden, but was out of luck because the dogs and I rushed out of the house and pursued it up the garden path.

There were a couple of sad notes, even among all the joy. A female blackbird caught her leg in a rat trap and lost her foot. The first thought was that she would die of shock, but she coped with her adversity well, and remained with us for another three years, hobbling around on her stump. Meanwhile, Bonnie ate a baby bird. We know this because she threw up the unrecognisable bloodied remains on the lounge carpet later that day.

Finally, a girl name Charlotte phoned from the production company to tell me that filming on the 12th of next month will start at 10.30 am instead of 8.00 am. I don't know what they're going to find because the wind is playing havoc with the taller plants, and the rain is turning the grass into a muddy mess again as the dogs run all over it. It looks like a ploughed field. The project was turning ugly.

EIGHT

JULY

There was a little time before the next filming day so it was time to go and steal more ideas from other NGS gardens, so the first place on the agenda was the School House in Little Torrington. Now when a gardener mentions the word steal it is because gardeners are like sponges, they don't literally steal things, but they are kleptomaniacs when it comes to ideas.

While there, I met Jo Hynes, again. She seems to everywhere at the moment, a bit like the weather. This time she appeared preoccupied, as though something lay heavily on her mind. But after attracting her attention we chatted a little. She mentioned that the NGS gave lectures with PowerPoint presentations. This excited me somewhat because by coincidence, I had just such a thing ready because I was due to give evening classes at the North Devon College in Barnstaple. I had spent some weeks putting together and eight-week wildlife gardening course for them. She said that if I'm accepted then I'm to contact Miranda Allhusen, the Devon organiser, and tell her I'm available. As ever, I couldn't resist buying a plant. This time I came away with another cranesbill, "Buxton Blue" this time. They're good ground cover liking either sun or shade. Oh, and an aster of an unknown cultivar. Asters are valuable for late autumn colour and more importantly, are a late source of nectar for insects and butterflies.

The other garden on our "to visit" list this month was Gorwell House in Barnstaple, but it never happened. I managed to take a wrong turning and ended up at Barleycott Gardens at Blakewell instead.

I wasn't disappointed with the error though, because the garden turned out to be most delightful. It was started in 1995 and covered approximately four acres. Superb vistas went off in all directions and the garden was in different sections, one such was an area with a gazebo that resembled a classical temple! Seats were everywhere and at all pertinent points where there was something of interest or a good view to be had. This was reminiscent of a visit to Westcott Barton, which had numerous points of view and it was while sitting on a wooden bench type seat and looking at the stream that Bill and I saw a mason bee digging out the pointing on the masonry under a coping stone of the adjacent bridge.

I came away with ideas, as I knew I would. I needed to make the garden attractive to mason bees for a start, but also plenty of seats will be installed as will the creation of more interesting focal points. There are also two plants I shall be introducing into the copse; wild strawberries (they were like a weed in this garden) and dicentra (bleeding hearts, or our lady in a boat, or Dutchman's breeches, or lady's lockets, or lyre flower, or tearing hearts, or Chinese pants; take your pick of any of these.)

※ ※ ※

It was time to start preparing the garden for the next filming session. Jo Hynes had emphasised the leaf mould bin so I got my tools out and built a "bee hive" style bin with bits of six centimetres by six centimetre timbers for the frame, and feather board for the cladding. It looked quite good even if I do say so myself. The only thing was that it had to be dismantled and hidden away until filming was under way because it would add to the threat of the situation; will the garden be completed in time? It was of a modular construction so it fitted just one layer on top of the other. Finally, between us, Evelyn and I made the rush screen she wanted. This was to hide the dustbin and other unsightly utensils.

It was then onto the garden itself. This needed a slight reorganisation so plant moving was in fashion. The small *skimmia* from the front of the copse was removed and replanted in a large terracotta pot. It was a real struggle to drag it into the courtyard garden. Why it wasn't potted up in the courtyard garden itself is a mystery; some things are never thought through. While there I planted a lupin that Evelyn had managed to get cheap at Morrisons Supermarket. There were self-sown granny bonnets growing unrestrained in the copse so they had to come up. They're one of the most promiscuous flowers in the world; some plants have no morals. One of them went in the courtyard while the rest went into the cottage garden border. Finally, after clearing a few non woodland weedy things out of the copse, the flowers we bought at the School House the other day were eagerly planted out. First the cranesbill went in a little way from the edge, and then the woodland aster went a little further in. It's a creeping woodland cultivar called *Aster divaricatus*, although the taxonomists have got hold of it and renamed it *Eurybia divaricata* for some reason. Finally, the *Ajuga reptans* (bugle) that came from the Cherubeer gardens found its place at the front of the copse. There was a tiny fern in the pot with it. How the dear little thing was clinging on to life is beyond knowing.

✧ ✧ ✧

Two days before filming though, an incident occurred that could have ruined everything. While at work and decorating the office of the new manager who was due to start in a few days, I climbed back down the steps and misjudged the bottom, thereby stepping into the air. I came down with a straight leg onto the sole of my right foot and on impact I felt my knee joint compress. It was like a pile driver, the pain was excruciating. Initially, I ignored it as best I could, but during the course of the morning it began to throb and slowly swell. This was just after lunch, so I signed off and when home. However, by the next morning the joint was stiff and painful to walk on. I needed a walking stick to get around with.

Consequently, the load for the garden fell on my dear Evelyn's shoulders. She had to spend the day tidying things up for the next day's filming. It would be out of the question for me to do anything of a physical nature physical nature on filming day so I wondered what they would do. Then I had a brainwave.

✧ ✧ ✧

Jerry, Gordon, and Charlotte arrived at 10.30 am prompt. It was amusing that to begin with, they were bubbly and chirpy as youngsters are, but when they were informed about my damaged knee they became most perturbed. But then I played my brainwave card and injected a positive attitude back into them again. I suggested that they could highlight the jeopardy angle of the situation. Their faces instantly brightened as they cheered up and decided to run with it.

They started by filming in the newly completed courtyard garden. Following that they dragooned Evelyn into planting the native hedge in the vegetable garden cornfield area that Carol Klein had suggested during her last visit. To up-the-anti they captured me hobbling down to the garden with my walking stick and then standing looking into the vegetable garden and waving and pointing my stick like an orchestral conductor while giving directions to Evelyn. The planting was appalling. It was just a question of digging holes, putting the plants in, and back-filling. We used no compost or fertilizer. It certainly was no advert for a proper "how to do it" production. It's hardly surprising that it never made the final programme.

Changing tack completely, they led me down to the path adjacent to the greenhouse and began an interview. The camera was trained on me in close-up and Jerry began to discuss my bad leg. The sun was bright that day and it made my SpecSavers reactolite-rapide glasses go dark. This didn't please Jerry and so he asked me to remove them; which I did. Apparently, be-darken specs makes the interviewee look like a gangster, how cool is that? While waiting for Evelyn to return the filming and interview continued. Evelyn eventually turned up with my old standard pair that had huge lenses. It made me look like a balding owl wearing a cap. By the way, Jerry also asked to take that off; I felt naked without it. The team still weren't that happy so it was glasses off again. So, on the finished product that was aired, they were interviewing me in close-up, and one second I've no glasses, but a cap; the next second I'm wearing glasses with giant lenses and no cap; then after that, by the time the interview and filming were finished, I'm again wearing no glasses, and no cap. The last part wasn't included in the final cut; it must have been an editor's nightmare!

They were interested in the compromised situation we found ourselves in. They focused particularly on the fact that Evelyn was doing a lot of the work because of my crocked knee, and that it gave me more time to engage in my writing. To this end they filmed me in the doghouse, while Evelyn worked. Evelyn was in the foreground constructing the new leaf mould bin after destroying the old one, while I could be seen through the doghouse window typing away like billy-o.

They were finished with us after a few hours, but for the next two and a half hours they just wandered around the garden searching for wildlife and things of natural interest. They finished at five-thirty in the afternoon, which meant they had been in our garden for seven hours. But they hadn't finished then, because just as they were packing up, Gordon the cameraman saw a cricket on the pillar by the front door and filmed it from three different angles. Immediately afterwards it was hearty handshakes and air kisses all round. And then off they went to Swansea to film another garden.

❀ ❀ ❀

The televised final dialogue after editing went something like this. (Carol's voice over.) 'In Devon, Henry's biggest challenge was making sure his projects came to fruition, but an unfortunate accident has unfortunately left Henry out of action.'
(My interview – glasses off – cap on) 'I've hurt my knee. It's the worse possible time for it to happen, because shortly we've got the county organiser coming round to reassess the garden and we've still got all these different jobs to do. So we're in jeopardy really.'
(Carol's voice over.) 'Luckily for Henry, his wife, Evelyn, has stepped in and is on hand to help.'

(Evelyn's interview.) 'It's very frustrating for Henry because he can't get round and do things. He doesn't like to see me doing it. He wants to be really involved with helping, so he can't be very happy.'
(Carol's voice over.) 'But Henry's the eternal optimist, and rather than dwell on the fact that he may be facing a second rejection, he's adopted a much more positive outlook.'
(My interview – huge glasses on – cap off.) 'There is one advantage I suppose of having a crocked knee and Evelyn doing all the work. It means I can do a little bit more to my writing.'
(Carol's voice over.) 'In North Devon, time's running out for the budding wildlife gardener.'

That's all folks. That is the remnant of four hours filming!

❀❀❀

After all the excitement of filming, Evelyn and I thought it would be a good idea to make sure the actual tour worked out all right, so we invited members of our congregation to come and see the garden. We'd try a couple of dry runs.

The first dry run began at 2.00 pm on the following Saturday. The guests arrived in dribs and drabs to begin with and the occasion fell naturally into two tours. About eight came on the first tour with nine on the second, seventeen in total. There was good light hearted banter, and during the second tour one of our friends noticed a mullein moth caterpillar on a *Buddleia Davidii* "Dartmoor," so everyone got excited and fell into a good photography session. It was encouraging to see the wildlife coming in. It meant that my mission was working. And it also proved that the tour idea would work and that there was forty-five minutes of interest.

The second dry run was scheduled for the next afternoon. Again it fell naturally into two tours. This time there were eleven friends in total, plus their children. There wasn't quite so much rapport as yesterday, but Bill came up with the idea of planting someone in the tour party to ask all the relevant questions. That way the visitors would get the maximum benefit from the tour. He suddenly found himself with a job. The children got up to all sorts of mischief, as they do, but they were fascinated by the ponds and particularly the newts (effts as they were once called by the old countrymen.)

Our friendly local builder, Dave Jackson and his wife were among the visitors, and being the fine fellow and friend that he is, he looked at the prospective site of our new fence. We finally plumped for a feather-board type fence and he said he would start the following week. There was a sense of urgency creeping in. The final judgement was drawing ever closer.

Rosemary, one of our friends who are into absolutely everything, took ages to go round the garden and because of that effectively ended up with her own tour. She really does enjoy wildlife. We discussed being able to shrink and see small things. Rather than just trying to swallow the whole picture, it's good practice to focus in on something and become "macro-minded." Take for example the sunflower. It's so easy to stand in front of it and admire its overall size, shape, colour and form, but go macro-minded and look into the flower. It doesn't take long to see that the seeds aren't set in the head any old which way. They actually follow the Fibonacci sequence. And mathematically, that is the way to get the maximum amount of seeds into a given space. Look closer and it's possible to see even other tiny little creatures making a living in the flower head. Creation is truly remarkable.

We agreed that macro-mindedness could apply to our own gardens as well. Eventually, we shall all need to look at small things. We'll need to do this because we're losing gardens to land grab as more and more gardens are built on. And the types of houses being built today merely have small courtyard gardens, if that. The population growth of Britain is staggering, and they all need houses. Eventually, if nothing changes, this country will end up like Hong Kong or Singapore. After all, we're only a small island. Something will have to give; will it be people or wildlife? We all know the answer to that question don't we? But at what a cost, we will all begin to live impoverished lives. If we look at society in city life, we can see that it has lost touch with the real world. It lives in a detached bubble devoid of the natural world. So, we live on a small island that's getting even smaller, therefore we must reduce things in our mind to help wildlife. If we all have some form of wildlife planting in our courtyard gardens, no matter how small. It will help because even in the smallest garden there is room for wildlife friendly flowers, shrubs, or petite trees. This is essentially the philosophy of town gardening. No space must be wasted because it is at a premium. Every inch must serve some useful purpose.

At the end of the day, Evelyn and I sat down and analysed the last two days' proceedings. We concluded that the tour probably needs a larger sweep of things rather than just small details; these details can be gleaned by reading interpretation boards and plant labels set strategically around the garden. It would be good to focus on certain areas and their benefits for nesting, nectar, and such like. We noticed too that the courtyard garden continually slipped through the net and was overlooked. That needed to be addressed. And finally, we reckoned that the narration of the tour needed to be planned and written out properly.

❀ ❀ ❀

I don't know why I do it. There must be something pathological in me regarding plants and planting. The following day I went to Barnstaple in an empty Vauxhall Astra estate car and came back with a full Vauxhall Astra estate car. It was a round trip starting at St John's Garden Centre where I bought, wait for it: two big terra cotta pots to replace the one I reversed into and broke a while back, a striking red yarrow (*Achillea millefolium*) called "Fire King", a Lady's Mantle (*Alchemilla mollis*) for the mini copse, a couple of French lavenders with fern type leaves (*Lavandula dentata*), a cut price bumble bee nest box with a broken lid (but that wasn't insurmountable,) and a ball of twine.

B & Q was the next stop where into the back of the Astra went five rolls of turf at half price (for the hens and green roof,) a Shasta daisy, two bales of bark chippings, a sandstone stepping stone, and three new dahlias called "Fascination" (they have attractive dark foliage with a handsome magenta flower, but not so hot as the Bishop of Llandalf and the rest of the Bishop range,)

Finally, after coming home and offloading all that lot it was down to Jewsons where another five bags of shingle was acquired, and which the Lady of the Garden and I immediately laid in the courtyard and in front of the compost heaps.

With everything now to hand it was time to construct the green roof on the tool shed. On the day I decided to do it the skies had opened and it was pouring with rain so as the job progressed, I got muddier and filthier, and I hurt my knee again. It was painful as the turves were lifted onto the roof and manoeuvred around. It was two turves deep. The first layer was green side down; the top layer was green side up. Finally, a ten-centimetre-wide batten was nailed onto all four sides to keep the whole lot in place; the roof was sloping at a gravity deifying pitch after all.

Realising that the final filming session was dangerously close, only a few days away, I was spurred into action. The potted herbs were artistically arranged in the courtyard garden, not the best place to prosper I know, but the place had to be filled with something before filming. The old pot-bound golden coloured conifers were potted up into the two new big terra-cotta pots. That caused a re-arrangement of the pots in the terrace now these other plants had been moved. The idea was to make the pots look good by the back door much like the pot display that Christopher Lloyd created by his back door at Great Dixter. It's a big ask, but hope springs eternal in the human breast.

❀❀❀

Like a flower that slowly pushes its way up and blossoms to the world, likewise the garden appeared to be slowly fulfilling its purpose. This had been a month of wildlife discoveries in all sorts of ways. At the start of the month, I discovered the strangely attractive caterpillar of the Vapourer moth, a weird and wonderful fellow with red warts along its side with pale hairs sticking out, and four tufts of yellow hair like old fashioned shaving brushes sticking up along its back. It's difficult to imagine how such an exotic caterpillar can become such a dull triangular imago (adult). A yellow eyed, brown caterpillar with dull yellow chevrons along its side was discovered in the greenhouse on the tomatoes, but although I searched through all my butterfly and moth identification books and field guides, I came across nothing. I couldn't identify it at all.

It was noticeable that the rats were beginning to get rather procreative again, and we couldn't allow that, an unscheduled appearance would scare the visitors. One afternoon at least three of the little beggars were seen going about their ratty business. One of them was by the terrace, and two others were by the doghouse. Their blatant bravery never fails to astonish. They care nothing about man or beast. They just look you in the eye and then carry on their business as if you didn't exist; the little horrors, they needed to be fixed somehow. Being organic I drew the line at rat poison, and instead tried a product made of sweet corn cobs (after the maize had been removed of course. The label in the tub said that the product swelled up inside them, and not being able to vomit, starved to death. Not a nice death, but maybe preferable to bleeding to death internally by rat poison. Shortly after, a dead smell came from the potting shed; it lingered for a while and then it went. It wasn't given another thought until some months later when clearing out the shed I came across a dead rat. It was flat but looked and felt like it was mummified. It was hard as leather. The rat killer must have absorbed the fluids from the body and dried it out. I haven't seen anything like it before or since.

Many of the birds were extremely active with feeding their midsummer broods. A couple of the nest-boxes had been taken up, so we had a number of avian neighbours. The bird population was high because we continued to feed during the summer. Once upon a time this was thought of as a no-no, but the current opinion is that it takes pressure off the adults to find food for themselves as well as their offspring, thereby increasing the chances of more chicks fledging well. The starling numbers dropped though, regardless. They drift into the country side and just call in for breakfast in the morning on their way out, and then again at dusk they drop in for supper on their way back before they all join in a great murmeration and go to roost under the old medieval bridge that crosses the River Torridge and joins East and West Bideford. It's a beautiful sight and it never fails to make everyone catch their breath in awe at its wonder. I did notice however, that in the copse there had been another sparrow-hawk casualty. It appeared to be the remains of a collared dove. Sad as it may be, it must show that there is a healthy population of birdlife in the area or else it wouldn't waste its time here.

Moving down the scale to the butterflies and insects, I had a grand time with my camera. I photographed a juvenile "white death" crab spider, and Peacock, Red Admiral, and Small Tortoiseshell butterflies. I chased a red-tailed bumblebee (*Bombus lapidarius*) around until it settled and then got a nice shot of it. I felt quite proud of myself. Finally, a pretty little female Holly Blue butterfly came through laying her eggs on the ivy arch, but unfortunately I didn't have my camera with me at the time.

❀ ❀ ❀

At the end of the month an unexpected reprieve arrived. The production company phoned to say that they wanted to change the filming day to the following Friday. That was a gift; it gave us extra time in which to get a bit more done, especially with my gammy leg, which I must say was slowly improving. Strangely enough, all this communication was carried out by answer-phone; the marvels of modern science, eh.

To finish the month, there was a call from Jo Hynes to say that she would be calling with the county organiser, Miranda Allhusen, at 3.00 pm on Thursday to preview the garden before filming on Friday. They will tell yea or nay then. There were a busy couple of days coming up. It was now make or break time.

NINE

AUGUST

Jo Hynes and Miranda Allhusen were due to visit on the Thursday, so that gave us a short time to tidy up a few loose ends. After work on Wednesday, I finished the green roof by planting it with various sempervivum, crocus, and saxifrage cultivars. I must admit that the final effect was most attractive. The green of the turf with the textures and colours of these perennials pleased me immensely. I could hear what may perhaps be compared to the sound of the waves on Westward Ho! beach as Evelyn spread the gravel where needed. Shortly afterwards I heard her spread the remains of the bark chippings in the copse. Toto the terrier had taken a fancy to these chippings. He'd steal the stuff, run off onto the lawn with it, chew it, and then leave it spread all over the place. Evelyn pressed on courageously and finished painting the door and window frame of the potting shed. She ended the day by cutting the grass. My day ended by watering all the pots, a time consuming task if ever there was one. The sun began to set on two exhausted gardeners.

The next day, at 3.00 pm precisely, Jo and Miranda arrived to inspect the garden. They looked as though they had come to do some gardening themselves, what with jeans, casual tops, and working boots of course. Still, Evelyn and I had done all we could, but if it wasn't enough, then so be it. We stood on the terrace for a while as Jo apprised Miranda of the jobs that had needed to be done to qualify for acceptance. After a nodding of heads and a weak grin I lead them off on a garden tour to examine the hot-spots.

Jo was pleased with the much improved leaf mould bin which now resembled a beehive complete with a fitted roof, the compost heaps which were now respectable being tidily enclosed in bins made of old pallets, and the beds that were scrutinised earlier stood proudly, all in fine fettle.

Returning to the terrace Jo and Miranda went into close conversation while I arranged for a cup of tea for everyone. When I brought the tea out it was good news. They had accepted our garden for the NGS and would try and team us up with Stone Farm along the Alverdiscott Road. This was much to my disappointment. I would have preferred to be a stand-alone garden.

❀❀❀

Jeff arrived first. He had spent the night in the Durant House Hotel, but was quickly followed by the rest of the team. It was 9.30 am. Jo Hynes arrived at about 10.00 am in her sizable 4x4 RangeRover. We had an amusing twenty minutes or so because the producer wanted her to drive up the road and in one move swing her RangeRover into my drive. This proved to be a recipe for a mathematical joke. Take one large 4x4, one small driveway entrance, one narrow road, and one assorted collection of parked cars, and then try to swing the large 4x4 into the small driveway. There was no way it was going to happen. In the end they took a shot of her driving up the road, cut, waited for her to manoeuvre herself backwards and forwards until parallel to the drive and then filmed her driving straight in. They didn't film her trying to get out of her car. She could hardly open the door it was so tight to the hedge; the poor thing, it was very unglamorous.

We did the introductory shots and then slowly wove our way around the garden and went through the time consuming process of discussing the improvements and changes. With only one camera everything takes so long. We both stood in position, and were filmed from one angle while the first person said their part, then it's cut, and repeat the whole thing but filmed from another angle as the other person said their part. It was enjoyable though and we all had a chuckle about it.

Eventually, Carol arrived and did her bit. She stared out from the terrace across the garden like a spy as her opening scene was filmed. After that Carol and I did the filmed walk around the garden discussing the things I had achieved and the philosophy behind the garden. She was really impressed by the garden and expressed how much I had to teach gardeners about the wildlife situation and what we can do for it in town gardens.

We had lots of laughs too. She is a down to earth person and fame has done nothing to change her. She is truly a case of what you see is what you get. And her work ethic is second to none. She explained that she had hurt her collarbone but didn't want to let anyone down, and besides, after filming with us she was on her way to Redruth in Cornwall for another session of shooting. Finally, we went through the finishing touches where we were accepted for the NGS.

As a parting shot, Carol suggested that I collect seeds as the plants went over and then sell them to visitors for the NGS. So I shall.

✺ ✺ ✺

As I recall, the final cut after editing went something like this:

Carol stood next to me on the terrace and started the discussion. 'Henry, the day of the reassessment is here.' She paused. 'You don't look terribly nervous Henry. Are you apprehensive?'

I glanced at her and jokingly chuckled, 'Yea. I'm bricking it.'

Carol laughed heartily in return. There was a short silence and then she asked, 'What do you reckon the county organiser's going to make of it?'

'Well, I hope she's going to go a bundle on it really, because I've ticked all the boxes and done everything that's been asked of me.'

'I should think she'd love it. I mean, you've been a good boy haven't you?'

'I have.' I said, and smiled.

Carol's piece to camera:

'It's only half an hour before the county organiser arrives to reassess Henry's Garden. He's taken everything on board, all her suggestions, and the whole garden's looking terrific. It's absolutely buzzing with life and activity; and that's what it's all about, it's a wildlife garden. I only hope he's done enough to get him into that Yellow Book.'

Carol's voice over:

'Just four months ago Henry's town garden was full of great ideas, but now those plans have become reality. The unsightly compost heap has been cleverly tidied away, the shed's got a new grass roof, and even the wildflower meadow has bloomed.

The garden's looking magnificent, but Henry's chances of being listed in the Yellow Book still lie with assistant county organiser, Jo Hynes.'

Cut to Jo Hynes calling at the front door:

'Hello Henry.'

'Hello Jo, nice to see you. How are you keeping?'

'All right.'

'Excellent stuff.'

Cut to the beach area of the garden:

'The beach is in sunshine.'

'Yes. That really warms up and all the insects come to warm themselves there, and hidden in among the shingle there are actually hundreds of little wolf spiders, and all these little spiders come running out from underneath the stones and go hunting.'

'Fabulous.'

'Yes, it's a great thing to watch.'

Cut to the compost heap/leaf mould bin:

Jo opened the conversation. 'Ah, the compost heap; now that was a bit of a heap the last time I was here wasn't it?'

'Yes, it literally was. It was just a pile of old rotten leaves inside some chicken wire held together by some old metal poles.'

Jo pointed to the wooden bumblebee nest box I had perched on one of the rear corners of the bin. 'I love that bumblebee nest, that's terrific. I see that there's just one bee there.'

'Yes, he's frozen. It was a bit cold last night.' I joked.

Carol's piece to camera:

Carol: 'I do hope that things are going well. I mean Henry's done so much work and the county organiser's got a real smile on her face. She looks quite happy.'

Cut to the wildflower meadow:

'Gosh, hasn't that been successful?' Jo exclaimed.

'Yes.' I replied.

'The wildflower meadow, it's really standing well. Considering all the rain we've had it's standing really well isn't it?'

'Yes it is.'

'What have you got in it?'

'Well, where do we begin? Well, we've got white campion, and we've got our old friend the poppy over there, which is very popular with the bees.' I pointed my finger in the general direction. 'There's one just gone in there now; the white tailed.'

Carol's voice over:

'So is it a yes or no this time for Henry?'

Cut to the three of us sit at the table on the terrace:

Jo looked at me with a beaming face. 'I'm very pleased with it and would love to have you in the garden scheme.'

'Oh, thank you so much. Oh, I'm so excited.' At this point I gave a stupid laugh which I thought would be funny, but it just sounded daft.

Carol leaned across to me 'How does that make you feel Henry?'

'Well, I'm really excited. Like I say, it's something I've really worked hard on all season, and now it's come to fruition and been accepted.' I leaned back in my chair with an element of pride.

Carol gave a hearty grin. 'Well, congratulations. I'm thrilled to bits because I think this is a wonderful enterprising garden.'

I nodded in return, 'Thank you Carol!'

But that's not quite the end of the story.

❀❀❀

Two of our closest friends, Rosemary and Eddie Cooper, came round to view the garden. I must admit that I wasn't looking forward to it because I felt tired after the filming day, but when they arrived and we started talking about gardening and the sharing of gardens, it gave me a lift, and my enthusiasm returned. They spoke about the gardens they had made and enjoyed over the years and expressed their pleasure with the design of our garden because it made the site look and feel larger than it really was.

After a tour we sat back on the terrace with a cup of tea and a piece of cake and the conversation drifted onto what natural gardening is. We came to the conclusion that there is nothing natural about gardening at all. The very definition of the terms garden and gardening indicates that the place is a contrived and managed environment. If something is natural, it indicates that nature is left to its own devises and what it creates is in essence, natural. If we left our gardens alone for five years, the end result would be telling. On our return we would find it to be heaving with brambles, stinging nettles, ivy, and such like. These things in themselves are perfect for wildlife and wonderful to have in a garden, but in vast quantities are not much use for humans and are rather limiting for our relationship with our neighbours.

After all, even the countryside isn't natural; it's as contrived as a garden. England's beautiful patchwork of green fields and woodlands, and even moorland to some extent, is man made for his own use.

Really, natural or wildlife gardening is all about learning from nature, adapting it to fit our environment, and using that environment to encourage and support wildlife. There is a higher density of biodiversity in the average garden than many an acre of natural countryside. But, it doesn't mean that we let our gardens go to pot. Dandelions left to their own devises will seed all over the garden (and the neighbour's gardens too.) Natural gardening is aimed at getting the maximum amount of diversity in the smallest amount of space.

The conversation moved on to domestic animals and their place in the garden. These bring much pleasure and on the whole are useful. Take hens for instance. They supply us with eggs, guano that activates the compost heap beautifully, and they are delightful company. It is relaxing to sit with the hens walking around you. And if you talk to them they will respond with a comforting, gentle, soft motherly clucking sound. What with that, and listening to the constant buzzing of the bees and other insects as they go about their business on hot summer days, the effect can be most hypnotic.

We compared the differences between cats and dogs because they are the most popular of domestic animals. We decided that cats are a no – no. They are arrogant and insolent. They are sly, devious, psychopathic murderers who go for soft targets such as birds and mice rather than dealing with the real menace – rats. Not only that, they use the garden as their privy. Newly sown rows of vegetables become a bomb site as cats bury their excreta. Then, in areas where they've been more discreet, you have your hands in the soil and suddenly come across it in a most unfortunate way. In contrast, dogs are fun. They're all noise and bluster. They hunt rats with great intensity and focus, but only occasionally catch one. Our cairn terriers have such wonderful open characters, full of zest for life. They try to please, but in doing so get over excited and bark a lot. They are natural gardeners too. They thoroughly enjoy digging, especially when you've just planted something. Having said that, they relish planting as well, hoping that it will grow into something special. They plant bones and pig's ears. They may be hoping that they'll grow into bone or pigs ear trees, but it's more likely to let the object decompose a bit thereby making it easier to chew. The little horrors also believe that newly potted up plants are toys and made to be run off with, spread around the garden, and the pot chewed. But who cares? Dogs? We love them to bits. Cats? Pahh!

We reciprocated by going to visit them and their garden. When they bought the bungalow it came with a huge pond. Unfortunately, it contains fish. Therefore, it has minimal value for wildlife. Eddie had introduced newts, but they didn't last long. They were soon gobbled up by the fish. There were pond skaters present and a goodly quantity of whirly-gig beetles. That irked me a bit, we could never, never, never, get any of these little beasties to inhabit our pond. The only pond life we could muster was sub-aquatic. However, his herbaceous border was a treat and his sweet peas smelt delicious.

I picked up some ideas to try while in conversation. Next year I shall try to grow strawberries in raised grow-bags, grow some stinging nettles, either as a small patch or in pots spread around the garden, and find somewhere for a bog garden if possible. This visit re-affirmed my idea to develop a proper cottage garden border, although I shall not just focus on native flowers but more of an international flavour. After all bees and butterflies aren't xenophobes. Rosemary again suggested interpretation boards to explain the philosophy behind each area of the garden. So I shall use that idea on my NGS open days.

We visited another couple of other NGS gardens during the month. Firstly, we went to The Croft, at Yarnscombe. We could see that it had once been a magnificent garden but as the owners had got older it had gradually drifted away from them. Many of the paths had become overgrown and could not be accessed comfortably. There were many untidy corners in this garden, which, if they were in mine, Jo Hynes would have made serious comment. Still, having said that, I don't want to decry the garden, it was a nice enough one-and-a-half-acre site on the whole, and the sense of noble decay added a pleasing dimension of atmosphere.

They also had ducks. And on the way home, Evelyn said something that I wholeheartedly agree with. She said that livestock adds another aspect to the garden, be it ducks or hens. I know that Evelyn is fond of ducks but it is impossible for us to keep them owing to a pair of cairn terriers.

The other garden we visited was Westcott Barton. It was absolutely stunning. The borders were full of insect friendly plants.

The sedums were swarming with butterflies and bees. The plants were prevented from flopping over by the use of wicker pyramids. The vistas are excellent. There are streams and bridges in profusion, and the main river that runs through the garden is as clear and clean as any Hampshire trout stream. You could grow watercress in it I reckon.

While sitting on a seat made of a stone slab supported by two short lengths of rotting tree trunk I saw a leaf cutter bee taking bits of leaf into its nest that it had made between the stonework and concrete capping of the bridge wall. There were dragonflies in the fishless pond, and the demoiselle so loved by Dr Haig was plentiful as well. A heron was in the field beyond and how I wished I had a camera with an effective telephoto lens. There was an arbour of escallonia and ivy, a pleached lime drive and a pergola. A pergola is a must for us this year if possible. That could be our winter project. I must think about what wildlife friendly plants to grow in it.

❀ ❀ ❀

It turned into an eventful month in the wildlife front. One afternoon a sparrow-hawk flew into the garden like a Tornado jet, intent on finding some lunch amid the current garden incumbents of sparrows and finches. However, the house martins that lived under the eaves of a neighbouring property had other ideas. Like a squadron of spitfires, they bravely buzzed it and harassed it until it had had enough and left empty taloned.

On the butterfly front there was still a lot of activity. The cabbage whites were still mating with gusto as they relished the thought of their offspring munching into my brassicas. A diurnal flying moth came swiftly through the garden one afternoon. It didn't appear to be one of the humming bird hawk moth types, but it was quite large. Unfortunately, I could find no trace of it in any of my field guides. Our Chinese White Birch was attacked by a hoard of Buff Tip moth caterpillars merrily munching through the leaves. If they had been left they would have defoliated the whole tree. Therefore, after much thought, I made the heart rending decision to remove the majority, but leave a few to grow on. I took a photograph and then undertook the foul deed.

The Bumblebees were beginning to wear themselves out and die. As I walked around the garden during the month I discovered various corpses here and there, so I picked them up and added them to my burgeoning natural history collection.

We made a concerted effort to get rid of the rat that had been worrying the dogs for so long. We analysed that the thing was living under the step that leads down from the corner of the path and onto the terrace. I came up with the ridiculous idea of smoking the creature out. What could be more straight forward than that? The rat would run out and then the dogs would do what terriers do so well, and dispatch it. We collected together a few sheets of newspaper, a load of dry lavender, and some joss sticks. We set it all on fire and poked it into a gap underneath the step. The dogs became very interested and thrust their noses into the gap ready for the rat to run. Much sniffing ensued and much recoiling followed immediately after. They had inhaled the somewhat pungent perfume, which they didn't like one bit. They spent the next ten minutes wandering round sneezing the pong out of their little doggie noses.

They did get their reward though, because at lunchtime Bonnie noticed it on the terrace. She instantly sprang into action and as it ran for home, she caught it, despatched it, and proudly trotted around the garden with her prize. As he was still a bit of a puppy, Toto didn't get involved, but stayed close by while Bonnie did her work.

❀ ❀ ❀

As the month came to a close we were still watering pots, and troughs, and baskets, and the greenhouse. It's easy to see how the time was drifting away to now. Seed heads were beginning to appear. The late flowering Echinaceas and michalmas daisies were starting their end of season show, generously providing late nectar for the insects, bees, and butterflies. Early in the mornings a translucent, steely-grey sheen sat on the shrubs and taller flowers. It was merest hint of autumn yet to come.

TEN

SEPTEMBER

This month started in a bitter/sweet fashion. I found myself out of work. The care home where I worked closed down amid great bitterness. I had recently interviewed a singer to come in and entertain the residents and had arranged for him to start a couple of weeks later. A week before he was due to come he phoned me and asked if we had read the building application section of the local paper. He said he wouldn't be coming and recommended we read it. He said nothing more. I popped out to the local shop and picked up a copy of the North Devon Gazette and scanned the property development applications to see what he was talking about. And there, in front of my eyes and unmissable at the top of the page was a planning application to demolish the care home and build a housing estate on the site.

The next day I enlightened the manager about the situation and she was astonished. There followed a flurry of phone calls between her and the owner to establish what was going on. I could hear through the door that there were some robust conversations going on. Not that I was eves-dropping mind you; it was raised voices you understand. Later that afternoon we arranged a staff meeting and the manger sadly reported back to the staff that the owner had indeed put in the application and had cleverly turned herself into a property developer. The home would be wound up in a matter of weeks.

However, it turned out to be not weeks, merely days. On Friday of the first week in September, the owner told the manager that because all the rotas had been filled she wasn't needed the following week. The poor woman was ordered to clear her desk. To a person with any integrity this was despicable behaviour, so in a show of solidarity to the manager, I resigned, and cleared my desk as well.

So that was the end of my part time job. Still, I didn't really mind. I was now free to pursue my own pursuits, albeit now financially poorer. The ones I really felt sorry for were the residents. They only had days to relocate, and it was truly upsetting for them. Some of them had been settled there for many years, and ranged from those who were residential to those who had severe dementia. It was a traumatic period for everyone concerned; except the owner of course who was laughing all the way to the bank. It would be best not to say any more about this episode; least said soonest mended.

❀ ❀ ❀

One morning I received an email from Jo Hynes, the assistant county organiser. She informed us were to be a joint opening with a farm along the Alverdiscott road. So she asked for the pink individual garden application form to be filled out with some urgency (like that evening.) To finalise the arrangements, we agreed to meet at Stone farm at five o'clock that afternoon.

The meeting was not good; there was tension between us from the start. From the very beginning we could genuinely say that they were not our sort, particularly the wife. All the time a sense of superiority and self-importance filled the air. If she was given half a chance she would have tried to take the lead and become the group co-ordinator, but there was no way that was going to happen. So while she filled out her pink application sheet, I made out the blue group garden application form.

We then had to discuss what title to give the group. Considering the tension in the atmosphere this could have lead to disagreement but I set my jaw, held my peace and decided to let it rest. I put forward the name, the East The Water Group; after all, it was the official name of the area in which we lived. The farmer's wife didn't like that. She insisted that we call the group, Bideford East. She felt that East The Water was a rather common sort of place, and Bideford East sounded much more posh. Her pride was pouring from every pore.

I will say no more on this, but I think you get the picture. Besides, they did not really do their own garden anyway. They employed a professional gardener to do it for them.

We finally agreed to open for three days; one day in May, one in late June, and one in August. Unfortunately, they were all Sundays, no bank holidays (which we would have preferred.) So that was another compromise on our part. And all the while Jo Hynes sat there as though a restrained referee. Eventually the meeting broke up and we left the farmers to themselves. We were not sorry to leave and drove away with a sense of relief.

❀ ❀ ❀

This month is effectively the beginning of the wind down to the gardening year. Everything is looking as though it's had enough and just wants to rest for a few months. Between now and October is the time for any last minute transplanting or planting before the winter sets in. It gives plants just enough time to get their roots growing and to settle in.

In the border of the driveway, after much swinging of the mattock and thrusting of the spade, the root of the Russian Vine was finally removed. It was humongous, but hopefully after all the bullying treatment it should be dead now. We lived in hope that there are no rogue roots hiding away just ready to jump out on us and attack us like an undead horticultural zombie

I gratefully took the opportunity to dig over this now vacant bed that stretched from the already planted three cherry plums to the elder near the gate. After giving it a good feed of compost, the lady of the garden planted the three remaining cherry plums to complete, what we hope will be a fine hedge. She found some unknown bulbs in the trailer and planted them in the border as well, as some sort of under planting. Oftentimes gardening is a glorious voyage of surprise and discovery.

Having cleared the terrace bed of the summer's show of antirrhinums we were at a loss of what to replace them with. So we went for jaunt to St John's garden centre for some inspiration and returned home with twenty-four modules of Sweet Williams. The previous year we had enjoyed wallflowers before the antirrhinums, but were loath to have them again because being members of the brassica family we didn't want to risk club root. Not only that, if left, the flowering quality of wallflowers diminishes year on year, until they become sad specimens of flower hood.

Having a rare spare moment, we decided to visit RHS Rosemoor. It is no more than a fifteen-minute drive, but as is usual, even though we are members of the RHS, we don't visit as often as we should. It was a relaxing delight. We had a sandwich, walked around the art exhibition, and viewed the winners of the RHS photographic competition.

The RHS are a cunning bunch; they know a gardener's weaknesses. To get out, visitors have to leave through the garden centre and toolshop/bookshop/gift shop/make you spend your money shop. So you know exactly what I'm going to say before I even utter a word don't you? That's right. We came home with two Michaelmas daisies, a dwarf sea holly, and a scabeous at 50% off.

While there, we discovered a remarkable wildlife plant, or rather, shrub. It's called *escallonia bifida*. It can be a little tender in Britain, but it can tenaciously survive westcountry winters. From a distance it seemed the plant was physically active. And it was. It was literally heaving and pulsing with bees, butterflies, and all manner of insects stocking up on early autumn nectar. We had never seen anything like it in our lives. I determined to get one at the earliest opportunity. Except that I got two. Shortly after our visit to Rosemoor, I was surfing the Internet and arrived at the Duchy of Cornwall's website. There was escallonia bifida in all its glory. They were very expensive with ridiculous postage costs, but I could not resist it.

Now, with early autumn upon us, and with next year's opening in view, it was the perfect opportunity to recreate the cottage garden border. It was slowly taking the form of a traditional cottage garden border, but with one or two red campion thrown in for good measure. We decided that, in the spring, we were going to be ruthless. We were going to root out the corn-cockle and the love-in-a-mist, but there will be teasels and foxgloves. Hopefully there should be a full season of interest coinciding with our open dates next year.

The left hand side of the path running along the apple and pear avenue was to be a mixed 'hedgerow'. In the bed were a number of poor specimens of scrawny scrubby shrub things. It was hard graft removing them, I'm sure their roots were fixed to the underside of Australia. We had a plentiful supply of ground elder growing there too. The introduction of that pernicious plant was one of those things we can thank the Romans for; although it does make good eating apparently.

The site was dug over, and as many of the old roots and ground elder roots as could be removed were removed. The bed was then covered with a goodly depth of home-grown compost from our new NGS approved feather-board compost bin; hurrah! Two lovely big planting holes were dug; one was for the dark leaved elder that's been struggling away in a pot underneath the Schumach all summer, and the other hole for one of the highly prized escallonia bifida. A sedum was removed from the wicker basket by the pond and planted between these aforesaid fellows. To finish off, four primroses were planted under the hawthorn to herald the spring at this end of the garden.

Finally, on the planting front, the cold frame was transferred to the vegetable garden so as to grow earlier and protected crops. While there I collected seed to sell at next season's open days. These comprised corn camomile, corn marigold, charlock, field poppy, and corn flower, not the cultivated cornflower variety, but the wild type, the type that doesn't get mildew. Whether to make a seed mix or keep to single species would be decided later. A mental note was made to remove the corn-cockle before it self-seeded everywhere. I forgot as usual.

❀ ❀ ❀

We found that a little bit of pruning was necessary. Now I hate pruning because I always feel that I'm disfiguring the poor plants. Every time I do it I have to bolster up courage to make that first cut, even though ultimately it's for their long term good. Conversely, the lady of the garden enjoys pruning with a passion. Give her a pair of secateurs or loppers and she would clear a rainforest in an hour. She was really getting stuck into the escallonia hedge one afternoon, when I managed to convince her, over a cup of tea, that maybe it would be a good idea to leave it a little longer because it was still flowering and the bees were still using it. Evelyn went on to do other pruning jobs. Not too sure how wildlife friendly the end results were, but hey ho, there we go. Never argue with a woman who possesses sharp gardening tools.

The cotoneaster that grew alongside the wall of the beach area had put on tremendous growth. It was now arching over that wall and, like an umbrella, was overshadowing the courtyard bed on the other side. It had to be pruned because it was causing the plants in that bed to draw forwards and become limp and dangly. Every cut thrust a knife into my heart. It pained me because I was stealing winter food from the birds by removing all those berries. I felt a traitor to the wildlife gardening cause.

Next on the agenda was the shrubbery that was going to be converted into a copse. The starting point was the ceanothus at the end of the terrace. It was adjacent to the bird-feeders and the birds enjoyed hopping and flapping about in it so there wasn't too much ruthlessness shown in the pruning handiwork. The poor old *Vibernum Bodantense* "Dawn" was next for a bit of hairdressing. A few limbs were lopped off it but I'm afraid that it ended up more holey than righteous. Although it had opened it up more and let in extra light, which was a good thing.

126

There was a delightful shrub on the corner of the copse and the path that needed attention. I think it was a *Prostanthera Cuneata* (Alpine Mint Bush) or something like that. It carried beautiful white Schizanthus type flowers in profusion held against a British racing green leaf mass. I was game just to tip the ends off but Evelyn was adamant that it should be dealt with robustly because it keeps pushing people off the path (metaphorically speaking of course, not literally.) It always grows back strongly so there was no real need to be concerned, but that's me. Finally, a young hazel was coppiced, and the summer pruning of the apples and pears was finished at last.

Of course, all this involved everything I hate; pairs of shears, loppers, and an extendable lopper that was totally uncontrollable and waved about while I tried to deal with the length of cord that is supposed to operate the blade, plus a pair of wobbly steps. Fortunately, the Lady of the Garden was coerced into doing all the high reachy stuff while I held the ladder. There was a price to pay for that though. There was a constant cascade of twigs, leaves, and various other wooden items with attached foliage falling upon me. Camouflage was the fashion of the day.

There were a number of dumpy bags full of prunings, so I thought the shredder would enjoy the first airing it had seen for years. The shredding began with the first dumpy bag. After a whole morning of high decibel shredding and the consequential ringing in my ears, it was finished. The whole bag had yielded a mere large rubber trug and a half of woodchips and leaves. It was no use for mulching, it was much to fine, but it would be alright for the compost heap. So there it went.

❀❀❀

Little did I know it, but there were consequences to pay for all that pruning. I certainly wasn't going to carry on with the shredding. The return for effort and time wasn't worth it. So now our trailer was behind the car and loaded to the gunnels with three dumpy bags and two fertilizer bags full of prunings. We also managed to fill the green wheelie bin to the max.

While unloading the prunings at the re-cycle centre we had the serendipitous fortune to notice a few sections of sawn up conifer tree trunk that someone had not yet thrown into the skip. After a short negotiation with one of the staff and a donation, we came away with them and a wooden folding chair that Evelyn though would be aesthetically pleasing, and a long handled trowel that I thought would be useful.

After arriving home, we removed the trailer and put it in the driveway rather than in the courtyard as we normally would do. Then, reversing the car into the drive, Mr Muggins here forgot about the length of the trailer's towing arm so connected with it and pushed the trailer backwards into yet another of the ill-fated huge terra-cotta pots, shattering it to pieces. It held a small golden conifer. Or rather it had held a small golden conifer. Fortunately, I had somewhere to plant it though, at the end of the terrace bed. Oh dear, the unforeseen consequences of pruning.

❀ ❀ ❀

One afternoon, the pair of us went to Fremington and bought a good hardwood garden seat at a very reasonable price that we had seen for sale in the Bideford Gazette classified adverts. That evening it was assembled and we were pleasantly surprised to see just what a handsome thing it was. That encouraged us to rearrange the seats that we already had.

The next day we moved the well (not a real one obviously) into the vegetable garden. The Lutyens style bench was moved to where the well was, the seat at the front of the conifer hedge was moved to the rear of it, and the new seat took pride of place at the front. Our philosophy is that a garden just cannot have too many seats, especially if it is open to the public. Not only that, I might like a sit down from time to time myself.

❀ ❀ ❀

One day we fancied visiting a garden and so looked through the Yellow Book and by great coincidence saw that Carol Klein's garden was open for the NGS. Unable to resist that one we decided to go and see it. We took with us, our friend Bill, and a couple of other friends, Anne and Viv Perrin. It was in the middle of the country close to the hamlet of Umberleigh, and we had to park the car in a field and walk down a long track. Thank goodness it was a dry day, if it hadn't been it would have been a rather unpleasant mud bath.

Carol recognised me straight away because of my cap, and welcomed us with great enthusiasm, as is her outgoing and gregarious nature. With Carol it truly is, what you see is what you get. We spoke often as she dashed back and forth talking to various visitors. She really does have a "to do" list type of mind. All the time Carol was dealing with numerous people and fielded a multitude of questions about plants and problems at the same time. She was a fine example of multi-tasking.

Carol's garden has an ideal position; it is on a slope that faces south, so has the sun most of the day. The main part of the garden was terraced, with large raised beds made of stone and wide paths running between them. The beds themselves were a riot of colour with all the late summer/early autumn flowers doing their business. There was a vibrant mix of Rudbeckia and Michaelmas daisies overflowing from the beds with wall upon wall covered by the fabulous Mexican daisy, so loved by Gertrude Jekyll. But above all, it was throbbing with insects, bees and butterflies – life! It was essentially a wildlife garden.

On the left, running the entire length of the site was an inviting, but small woodland area with a stream running all the way through it. Carol said that it is primarily a spring woodland, with a carpet of colourful woodland plants.

When it was time to take our leave, we bought two Rudbeckia, a glorious bright yellow yarrow, and a few seeds. Seeing us about to go, Carol caught up with us again and she gave me some fresh vibrant new seeds, seeds that should have a generous germination rate. We had a kiss goodbye (not everyone can say they've been kissed by Carol Klein) and made our way out.

Going along the track we met Dr Haig, who was coming in as we were going out. He recognised me, but couldn't put a name to the face until he remembered his nick-name for me – King Henry! He was his usual effusive and bouncy self, and he always leaves a person with the impression that meeting you had made his day. Little did he realise that it was the visit to his wildlife garden two years previously that lead me on the road to opening a wildlife garden, albeit rather smaller than his.

❁❁❁

The dogs made us aware that we had another active rat on the terrace. No doubt it moved in to fill the vacancy left by the previous occupant whom Bonnie despatched a while earlier. To try and stop him we went through all sorts of contortions. Firstly I removed the euonymus that was next to the steps and stuck in a pot. I then lifted the first step and cleaned out its setting. There were rat runs galore so to combat their subterranean excursions the runs were blocked with stones. I set the slab back in place with 'Hard as Nails,' a wonderful all-purpose adhesive that will stick anything. I used more 'Hard as Nails' to fill the gaps, and rubbed sand into it to dull its brightness and to give it texture. Job done, I replaced the euonymus with a juniper 'Skyrocket' from the courtyard thinking that it could make a good structural impact. I found some old 'Forget Me Not' seeds and sprinkled them around for good measure hoping for a fine show from them the following year. Two days later there were piles of earth, stones and little entrance holes leading under the first step. The darn rodent was in there again. It must be a truly desirable residence. I would just have to wait until Bonnie and Toto could do the business once again.

❁❁❁

Midway through the month we enjoyed a visit from the press. Graham Andrews, the semi-retired gardening correspondent of the North Devon Journal, our local weekly newspaper, came to visit.

He arrived at 10.30 in the morning and we enjoyed a pleasant chat over a cup of tea. We discussed the NGS, our opening dates, the filming, and the reason why we were doing wildlife gardening. It was interesting that Graham was really old school because he took his notes in shorthand. He felt that tape-recorders were unreliable and prone to breakdown at inconvenient times. He took one of my tour leaflets for extra information.

I gave him a tour of the garden and fortunately there were plenty of interesting plants still in bloom. I explained the different areas of the garden and what they were about. For photographs he had me stand in the middle of the summer wildflower meadow, and then in the cottage garden crouched on my haunches behind a dahlia "Fascination," (no easy feat for a fatty like me.) He then photographed a hoverfly on a sedum, and the berries on the cotoneaster. He was here for a good hour and a half. Still, it would be interesting to see what he has would write about the visit and the conversation we enjoyed. He says that you only need about three megapixels for newspaper publication photos, which was useful to know.

❀ ❀ ❀

One afternoon, late in the month, Evelyn and I sat in the garden with a cup of tea and ruminated over the last few weeks' observations.

There were plenty of spiders in evidence; it was that time of year. They were building up energy reserves to see them through the winter. Now I don't mind spiders eating flies, but I do draw a line at bumblebees. There was a small one caught in a web that was stretched across a *verbena bonariensis*. Bigger bumblebees are usually big enough bruisers to battle their way out of a web, but this little fellow was struggling. Therefore, with a thin twig he was eased out. With that, he was away without too much hassle or loss of pride.

The garden was certainly fulfilling its purpose. It had welcomed every one of the six most common species of bumblebee in Britain during the summer. They are known as the "Big Six," *Bombus terrestris* (Buff-tailed bumblebee,) *Bombus lucorum* (White-tailed bumblebee,) *Bombus lapidarious* (Red-tailed bumblebee,) *Bombus hortorum* (Garden bumblebee,) *Bombus pratorum* (Early bumblebee,) and *Bombus pascorum* (Common carder bee.) But, for all its hard work, the poor bumblebee has a sad end. In late summer the nest breaks down as new queens fly off and look for somewhere to hibernate. The remaining bees have nothing to do but idle around like aimless teenagers. As there's no nest to take pollen back to they just feed themselves and fly about until they wear themselves out, or until the weather becomes so cold that they die of hypothermia.

But, there was also a seventh bee. When looking to see how the cherry plums were doing along the driveway, I noticed perfect half-inch semi-circular cut outs on many of the leaves. That meant that a leafcutter bee (*Megchile centuncularis*) had been busy that summer. I wondered where she had been making homes for her children.

And an eighth was in evidence too, the honey bee (*Apis mellifera*.) Someone nearby must have had a hive. There is no doubt that honey bees are one of the most important insect pollinators in the world because they will only collect pollen from a single species of plant when on a foraging trip. This reduces the chance of foreign pollen being carried to the next flower. If you want to tell the difference between male and female honey bees, the males have large eyes.

There was still plenty of bird activity. Colourful blue tits were ever twitchy and alert. Dazzling chaffinches were timidly landing on the feeders, grabbing a sunflower seed and then darting away. It gave the impression that the poor things were intimidated by the local quarrel of sparrows that live in Sparrow Terrace. Most beautiful of all though was the charm of goldfinches that regularly come through the garden and feed with gusto on the nyger seed supplied for them. There was much falling out and wing-flapping across a real mix of generations and gender.

There was an Ichneumon fly present as well. This is another positive sign that the garden is going in the right direction. This is a parasitic fly that lays its eggs next to the Horntail wasp larva which lives in decaying timber (hurrah for the log-pile.) She does this with a drill-like ovipositor which is as long as her body, if not even a little bit longer. And with orange red legs she looked positively prehistoric.

After a while we took Bonnie and Toto for a walk in the fields at the end of the road. The new housing estates were gradually eating their way through the fields and soon all these lovely amenities will be gone under the heavy weight of housing expansion. Nature continues to be pushed aside and put under even more pressure to survive. It just goes to demonstrate how important it is that the mantra of wildlife gardening in the urban landscape is repeated as often as possible.

✿✿✿

For tens of generations we have become brainwashed against certain flowers known as weeds. But what is a weed exactly? Traditionally, a weed has been thought of as a plant growing in the wrong place. And this is true; I have tried all manner of means to come up with a better definition but have been unable to. But, by that yardstick, it means that even if the most beautiful, delicate, and rare flower was growing where you didn't want it, then in all honesty, it's a weed. But what if you had a plant normally referred to as a weed, say, the common fumitory, growing in just the right place, then it's not a weed. But, you may be inclined to pull it up because we have been conditioned to do so. Alternatively, if you want to grow stinging nettles, they aren't weeds. You made the conscious decision to grow them. Still, it doesn't mean that we need not be cognisant of which wild flowers to grow in the space we have. As mentioned previously, we have had some real battles with plants such as the flag iris. They had to be evicted. We quickly discovered that corn-cockle had that trait so we decided to limit its place in the garden. So what is a weed? Well, the answer is pretty subjective. Is a weed what you want it to be, or not to be? That is the question. Sorry Shakespeare.

Today, wildlife gardening is about changing our gardening philosophy. We need to throw off the dictates of fashion, tradition, and snobbery. We need to develop an artist's eye and be appreciative of creation. It's good to see the beauty and value in things for what they are. Ivy, thought of as a weed, comes in a variety of types. It adds strength to the garden. It's a natural climber and will cover a shed wall, an archway, a house wall, in fact any vertical space. As explained in my letter to The Times newspaper, if the rendering or pointing is sound, then ivy will not damage house walls, rather, it protects them. It's essential for insects, butterflies, birds, and is beneficial as potential roosting sites. It does need controlling, but so do other climbing shrubs such as Virginia creeper and *Garrya elliptica*. And of course, all these ideas about bedding exotics and border fanciness are a hangover from the Victorian/Edwardian days of Loudon and Jekyll et al. Again, it doesn't need to be like that, it's all a matter of taste, but the wildlife garden can be as simple or as complicated as you like.

It can't be stressed enough that the basis of wildlife gardening is being organic. A garden's ecology revolves around an intricate food web. Simply put (although it's much more complicated than this) vegetation is at the bottom, pests are in the middle and predators are at the top. Pesticides, fungicides, and herbicides are poisons. And if they poison the garden, they will poison you too. Once used, you become a slave to them. They kill both predator and prey which breaks the web and leaves a dangerous vacuum. But, once you stop spraying, the pests come back with a vengeance because there are no predators to keep them in check. It takes a bit of bravery to wait three years for the balance of nature to reassert itself, but it's oh so worth it. It's much more satisfying to hear the buzz of bees and witness the activities of insects and birds on a warm summer's day than to just hear the garden's silence and traffic noise coming from the main road. A garden must be organic to be a real success.

❀ ❀ ❀

The programme was finally aired just after lunchtime on the 27th. The family sat around and seemed to enjoy it. Mother beamed as she saw her boy on television, and my brother and sister were totally unmoved by the whole thing as is their usual attitude to most things in life.

The programme covered two gardens in half an hour. With much cutting back and forth each garden had quarter of an hour each. It is surprising how twenty-four hours of filming can be reduced to fifteen minutes' air time.

It must be said though that the whole episode was a great education and an exciting experience. We met famous people, gained insight into how the television industry operated, and proved to ourselves that we could have a garden fit to show people. But, most importantly of all, we confirmed that it is possible to create a sustainable, organic, wildlife garden in an urban environment. If, by opening to the public for the NGS in future years, we manage to make at least just a few converts to the wildlife cause, then all the hard work and worry will have been worthwhile.

APPENDIX

A GARDEN TOUR

Now it would hardly be well mannered of me to let you go without a tour of the garden would it? Therefore, in this appendix (not a body part, but an addendum) you can see the plan of the garden and read the interpretation sheet supplied to our visitors during our first open year.

THE GARDEN PLAN

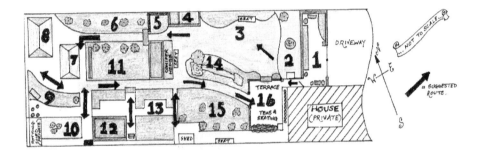

CHERRY TREES WILDLIFE GARDEN

BIDEFORD – DEVON

THE COURTYARD GARDEN: (Area 1) The idea behind this garden is to demonstrate that just because some people only have a small courtyard garden, such as we find in the new-build houses of today, they too can be made attractive to wild life.

The principle is just the same as gardening for wildlife in a larger space. It is good to choose the right plants, those that supply copious amounts of nectar and flower for a long period. Also, it is good to try and extend the flowering season for as long as possible.

136

Use vertical space as well. Grow plants that hug walls such as winter jasmine. Put trellis on the wall too. If mounted on blocks of wood birds will build nests there. This will happen when the climbers have woven their way through the trellis and thickened up. Hanging baskets and wall baskets planted with nasturtiums, antirrhinums, sweet peas, fuchsias, and such like will be great attractants.

Just because the courtyard is small that doesn't mean it precludes water in the garden. There will always be room for a birdbath. And if there is a vacant space on the wall, why not install a lion mask water feature, or even a pebble pool on a paved area. Water will always attract wildlife.

And of course, nest boxes should be put up for the birds to roost and breed in. If you can run to it, a nest box camera will be great fun and will bring many hours of pleasure.

THE LAWN: (area 3.) If there is space for a small lawn it is beneficial to the ecology of the garden, but not if manicured to within an inch of its life. Let the grass stay a little lusher, grow a little longer, be a little ragged at the seams. Your local wildlife will love you for it.

WOOD PILES: (area 5.) Here there are log piles surrounding a thin old mountain ash. There should always be plenty of rotting wood in the garden. If you don't like its somewhat acquired aesthetic appearance, you can hide it discreetly behind shrubs or suchlike. Rotting wood is of great value to generations of invertebrates and other beneficial creepy crawlies.

WATER IN THE GARDEN: Water is probably the most important habitat for wildlife. This is yet another environment that is under serious threat because since the middle of the last century, wetlands have been filled in, drained, or left to silt up. Fortunately, gardeners can come to the rescue by putting water in their garden. Water is vital to life. Every living thing needs water in some form.

Water can be featured in all sorts of ways. And it doesn't have to be an ocean. Here at Cherry Trees we have a small beach (area 2) with a small round pond imitating a rock pool (use your imagination please). We also have a short mountain stream that runs down to another small pool (area 14.) It must be said though that the larger the pond the better. But even if your garden doesn't stretch to that, any area of water is better than none. Even an up-turned dustbin lid or birdbath will enhance the wildlife attracted.

Even though the pools at Cherry Trees are small, they support much wildlife. Newts, frogs, pond snails and the occasional pond skater populate them. Birds use the ponds to drink. Even the water butts support healthy colonies of Daphnia, Cyclops and mosquito (which the birds devour and feed to their chicks.)

The stonework of the stream area offers shelter to the amphibians. Sometimes on damp evenings, frogs can be heard croaking from under the stones. And these of course help to keep the ecology of the garden in balance by eating plenty of slugs and other pests.

Water in the garden is essential and its value cannot be underestimated.

DRY STONE RAISED BEDS: These were built by Evelyn as a project she had been contemplating for a while (area 4.) The larger of the beds contains an assortment of winter flowering heathers.
HEDGEROWS: Over the last 50 years or so 150,000 miles of hedgerow have been grubbed out and destroyed to make monoculture farming more 'efficient'. But the hedgerow is as important as the woodland edge, if not more so. The hedgerow is the main arterial route in which wildlife seeks shelter, nesting sites, food, and a safe passage from one wooded area to another.

There are numerous examples of hedgerows with others under construction here at Cherry Trees. The short length of conifer hedge at the centre of the garden is kept trimmed and thick and is a regular nesting site for dunnocks. Just behind the walled garden (area 13) is a stretch of bramble interplanted with Rosa rugosa; the rear wall carries ivy (food plant of the holly blue butterfly). Against the rear wall of the cornfield is a young hedge of holly, hawthorn, and cherry plum. Along the apple and pear tree walk (area 6) is a young hedge that will eventually be made up of elder, hawthorn, black elder, and mahonia.

None of these hedges are purist hedges because this is a small town garden (although we've had no complaints from the wildlife customers yet!), but if your garden were large enough to allow a proportion of it to go truly wild, then a traditional hedge of native plants would be the ideal.

If your garden is a small new build courtyard type garden then use climbers over arches or on the walls.

WILDFLOWER MEADOW: Here is a shocking statistic… Britain now has just 2% of the unimproved grassland it had in the mid 1950s… a loss of 98%! Wildflower meadows were once the rural idyll. Rolling acres of flower filled grassland were quintessentially British. Every year the agricultural cycle of mowing and grazing kept the fertility of the land low so that the wildflowers could thrive. The increased use of nitrates and silage making instead of haymaking has been another cause of the loss. And as we would expect, these meadows were important habitats for all manner of creatures.

Gardeners can help though. No matter how small a garden we have, a space can be found for a wildflower meadow, be it a spring one or a summer one. As you can see, the one here at Cherry Trees is no larger than a sheet of hardboard (area 10). But it contains a surprising amount of species. There are: red and white campion, wild carrot, ox eye daisy, poppy, musk mallow, Ribwort plantain, sorrel, yarrow, cammasia and others.

Most success lies in starting from scratch, from bare soil, and sowing a seed mix of grass and wildflowers from a firm such as Meadow mania. This is what we did here. And to complete the effect we put in a small multi-stemmed silver birch. The results have been worthwhile. On hot sunny summer days, the meadow literally heaves with insects, butterflies, and bees. In the spring, even mining bees reveal their presence by making holes like tiny volcanoes in the soil.

If you want to convert a large area of lawn, mow for a couple of seasons, making sure to remove all the grass cuttings, and do not feed, then plant out wildflower plugs.

THE CORNFIELD: (area13.) Everyone knows the painting of poppies in the cornfield by the impressionist artist Monet. And just over half a century ago, the cornfields of Britain looked just the same.

> After World War 2 though, in an effort to make farming increasingly 'efficient,' the farming community made war against agricultural 'weeds' and applied powerful herbicides to eradicate them. In this, they have succeeded. Many of the old cornfield wildflowers are now virtually extinct in the wild and only exist because organic wildlife gardeners grow them in their gardens or smallholdings.

Some of the species to be found in cornfields are: Field poppy, attracts hoverflies, honeybees, bumblebees, and butterflies, birds eat the seeds. Corncockle (now a protected species in the United Kingdom) attracts bees and butterflies. Corn marigold attracts bees and butterflies. Cornflower attracts bees for pollen and nectar, butterflies for nectar, and blue tits and finches for seeds. Nipplewort, (every seed of this seems to germinate). Scented mayweed attracts bees, butterflies, and moths. And corn chamomile for insects, bees, and butterflies.

So as can be seen these wildflowers are important to the insects, butterflies, and bees that frequent the countryside. And the seeds of these wildflowers play an important part in helping to feed the birds during the long famine periods of winter.

If you don't want to go to the effort of making a wildflower meadow then take the easy option, create an annual cornfield instead.

THE VEGETABLE GARDEN: The vegetable garden is run on the bed system. This means that the soil is not walked on at any time and therefore is kept in good structure. The vegetable plant spacing is *very* loosely based on the square foot principle to maximise production from a small space. The vegetables grown are wherever possible heirloom varieties (those with a bit of history).

The birds seem to enjoy the vegetable garden as much as we do. They use the newly tilled soil for their dust baths and leave little saucer shaped indents all over the place. We tolerate it because it doesn't cause that much damage and they do need to do their toiletries. Our philosophy with nature is to live and let live as much as possible. The birds bring us more benefits by eating pests and grubs than any nuisance they may cause by dust bathing. Of course, if there is space, a couple of hens give added value to a garden by supplying guano to activate the compost heaps and lovely organic eggs (area 12).

GREENHOUSE: A greenhouse (area 7) is invaluable for getting a head start on the season and to over-winter the more tender type of plants. They come in all shapes and sizes these days and one can be found to fit even the smallest garden.

THE SUMMERHOUSE: The summerhouse (area 8) is where I keep my small natural history collection. It's not really an area for the faint-hearted but there is an interesting array of specimens for those so inclined. (This is also where I write.)

THE SUMMERHOUSE BED: This is a bit of a wild bed (area 9) with stinging nettles, dogwoods, lords and ladies, primroses, cowslips, a couple of clematis, a Philadelphus, and an elder called 'Chinese Lace.'

THE COTTAGE GARDEN: This is one of the most important beds in the garden (area 11). This is the nectar bar for all those wonderful bees, butterflies, hoverflies, and other insects that look after your patch. This is the attractant for your organic flying living pesticides! Plain and simple open type flowers, annual, biennial, and perennial, will satisfy the hunger of the most epicurean of flying creatures. Try and have as long a flowering period as you can possibly create.

THE WOODLAND EDGE: The woodland edge (area 15) is one of the most richest and important habitats for wildlife. But over the last 50 years, we have destroyed more woodland than our ancestors did in the preceding 400 years. We can re-dress the situation by converting our shrubberies to woodland edges.

The woodland edge shrubbery here at Cherry Trees is currently under construction by gradually removing some of the non-natives and slowly introducing more plants that are indigenous. There is no reason why non-natives should be excluded unless you are a purist but any that are included should be wildlife friendly and 'earn their keep'.

Essentially the woodland edge has tallish shrubs and trees as the upper layer. In a small to medium garden setting, tall shrubs such as the elder and hawthorn will fill the role well if left to mature. Hazel is a useful addition and can be coppiced for pea and bean sticks (and you get nuts!).

The middle layer should comprise smaller shrubs. Here we currently have skimmia (which supplies nectar to early flying bumblebees) and *Vibernum Bodantense* 'Dawn', which again, early-flying bees love.

The understory is made up of wildlife friendly plants suited to the situation. Here we have, amongst others; hellebores, white dead-nettle, buttercup, bluebells, red campion, ferns, a woodland aster, wild daffodils, Alchemilla mollis, cyclamen, herb Robert (our wild geranium) even the wonderfully scented violet oderata. The leaf litter (and added bark chippings) create the ideal place for creepy-crawlies, which of course are food for the blackbirds, thrushes, and robins.

THE TERRACE: (area 16.) This is the place for a cup of tea and a slice of cake, and a jolly good chat about wildlife gardening. Please sign the visitors book when you leave, we are always looking for ways to improve so your comments are welcome.

PLEASE RETURN THIS INTERPRETATION SHEET WHEN

LEAVING THE GARDEN - THANK YOU.

Well, that's the tour of the garden, the garden as it stood on the first year of our opening for the National Garden Scheme. Should you find yourself in the vicinity of our garden during one of our open days please come along and see it for yourself. Of course a garden is not set in aspic, it's like a growing and developing organism, therefore it will no doubt not be exactly as described in the book or the tour given above. Things change every year. But then that's the beauty of gardening, it's never boring.

In conclusion, it's interesting to note that on the whole, the British are an insular race for the most part, and like to keep themselves to themselves. But the garden is something special to them. This is something they like to share. And each year, more and more people open their gardens for the National Garden Scheme. And each year more and more people visit them. It can become a bit of a hobby. It is huge fun showing and visiting. It's one of the greatest days out imaginable, and there's an NGS garden not far from you. Look it up in the Yellow Book and have a go, because not only will you enjoy yourself, but you'll be helping loads of charities into the bargain. How good is that?

Hello everyone, it's Henry! Just before you go can I have a word? …

Thanks for buying my book; I hope you enjoyed reading it. The Lady of the Garden is certainly glad that this labour of love is finally out in the open air, where we all should be. If you have any constructive comments, questions, or feedback, it would be great to hear from you. The only way I can improve is to act on the advice I receive from my readers. So please help me out.

You can contact me on my Facebook page: www.facebook.com/UpTheGardenPath.
OR
Through my website: www.cherrytreeswildlifegarden.weebly.com
OR
You could always email me at CherrytreePress@gmail.com

Finally, if you get five minutes, could you leave a brief review on Amazon? A couple of lines will be fine. Reviews are the life-blood of authors… and they are read, honest! Just find your way to Amazon.co.uk or if in America, Amazon.co.com and look for "UP THE GARDEN PATH." The rest is up to you my friends.
So to paraphrase what the fat lady (Janet Webb) said at the end of the Morecombe and Wise show each week… "I'd like to thank you for reading my little book. If you've enjoyed it, then it's all been worthwhile. So until we meet again, cheerio, and I love you all!"
blows kisses

Printed in Great Britain
by Amazon